NOW THAT YOU KNOW

A Journey Toward Earth Literacy

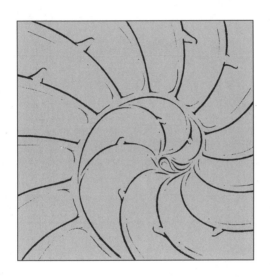

MCGREGOR SMITH, JR.
Foreword by Miriam Therese MacGillis

Earth Knows Publications
Washburn, Tennessee

Layout Design: Jerry Grotzinger
Illustrations & Cover: David Dimick

This book is printed on recycled paper containing 30% post-consumer waste.

Library of Congress Cataloging-in-Publication Data

Smith, McGregor, Jr.
    Now That You Know

    Bibliography
1. Man-Influence on nature. 2. Human ecology-Philosophy.
3. Environmental ethics. 4. Environmental responsibility.
5. Cosmology
1997   97-75235
ISBN: 0-9644659-7-3

10 9 8 7 6 5 4 3 2 1

For Helen, Sally, and the Council of Grandmothers

CONTENTS

ACKNOWLEDGEMENTS

This "seed book" has been a community endeavor. The following friends have had a hand in cultivating the manuscript: Norma Watkins, Tim McGuirl, Joyce DiBenedetto-Colton, Bob Tighe, Ross McCluney, Ted Keiser, Joe Iannone, Jody Bryan, Dan Daniel, Judy Smith, Jim Hodgman, Roy Fairfield, Elyse Rapaport, Robert E. Paige, and Bill Holden.

In its later stages, valuable assistance in editing was provided by Jack Gale, Anna Maria Caldera, and Sister Miriam Therese MacGillis.

In the final stage, I am grateful for the careful and considerate work of Earth Knows editor Daniel G. Deffenbaugh, and layout designer Jerry Grotzinger. I am also indebted to David Dimick for his fine illustrations.

All income from sales of this book, over and above the cost of printing, will be divided between the Narrow Ridge and Genesis Farm Earth Literacy Centers.

FOREWORD

To find my own story woven into the story out of which McGregor Smith weaves this book is one of the greatest honors I have ever received.

Few people I know have as brilliant a mind and spirit as Mac. From the first time I began working with him in Miami, I came to marvel at his capacity to take the most complex ideas and reduce them to their elegant simplicity in language and metaphors easily grasped. His genius is not only to capture an idea but to bring it to a place of synthesis and feeling that can excite and renew a weakened heart.

In this book, a chance encounter with a young boy evolves like a mighty oak from within an acorn. What was a powerful, brief experience has lived in Mac over these years and has in the process evoked the powerful potential of what the New Universe Story holds for an individual or culture yearning for meaning.

That this little jewel can find its way now to countless other seekers is a great gift. For students and mentors, for the old and the young, this deeply personal journey of exploring and living a new cosmology can open the future to hope, excitement, and a renewed opportunity for dreams.

Miriam Therese MacGillis
Genesis Farm
July, 1997

PROLOGUE

MY GRANDDAUGHTER CALLED ME WITH A MOUSE

Today my three-year-old granddaughter, Aubrey Elizabeth Larson, called me long distance with a mouse. She was excited. The mouse was a present from her mother. She used it to fish out my phone number from the family computer. She clicked on the number and, hundreds of miles away, my phone rang.

In the years to come, Aubrey Elizabeth will fish more and more information out of a vast electronic sea. She will know more than I will ever know, and perhaps more important than knowing, her mind will function differently. She will think in a "new manner."

Over half a century ago, Albert Einstein said that humans will eventually have to master a "new manner of thinking." My granddaughter is being prepared to leave behind the old paradigm, the obsolete worldview, one that Einstein claimed would inevitably lead to catastrophe. Her preparation is unplanned, unintentional, but she will one day emerge from the sea like a new species in the universe.

A human being is part of the whole called by us "universe," a part limited in time and space. We experience ourselves, our thoughts, and feelings as something separate from the rest. A kind of optical delusion of consciousness.

This delusion is a kind of prison for us, restricting us to our personal desires and to affection for a few persons nearest to us. Our task is to free ourselves from the prison by widening our circle of compassion to embrace all living creatures and the whole of nature in its beauty.

Albert Einstein[1]

INTRODUCTION

This is a story about how the universe uses grandchildren to overcome the roadblocks that we adults often put in their way. The path we will follow stretches backward in time at least 15 billion years. This is also a story about grandparents who, inspired by grandchildren, become pathfinders, those who, as Thoreau suggested, hear a different drummer. Pathfinders are often like fish out of water, aware that they are living in a world that doesn't make sense. It is a world out of touch with reality.

Children on Earth today are a little like fish out of water. At some level, children know that what they are being trained to do with their lives is meaningless. But the drummer of the universe is like another heartbeat within us, and the persistent rhythm will not allow us to rest. It is as if a tide stirs deep within the cells of our bodies, gently pulling us in a different direction from the one that has been foisted upon us.

The reason more of us do not turn and go where we are being called is that we feel imprisoned. Einstein was fond of this analogy, referring to our imprisonment as an "optical delusion of consciousness." We have been deceived, he said, into assuming that we can "experience ourselves, our feelings and our thoughts as separate from the universe." We are often urged to cultivate our separateness. We make it the basis of our education. We make our individuality our religion. But Einstein also knew that we can, and we must, free ourselves from the burden of such shackles:

> We must widen our circle of compassion.
> We must embrace all living creation.
> We must affirm the whole of nature in its beauty.

Long after I completed my Ph.D., and years after I moved from journalism to a career as a college professor, I found myself back in kindergarten. *Now That You Know* is a tribute to the teachers there who taught me how to get out of prison. The method was appropriate for grandparents like me, those of us who are presumed to have reached a certain level of maturity. It centered around story-telling. In kindergarten I learned a new story about who I am, and about what it means to be human. Almost all "the facts" I learned I already knew, but I had been perceiving them through the lens of "the old manner of thinking." I soon realized that nearly all of my education and professional experience had been shaped by a prison mentality, and this reinforced the delusion of my separateness.

THE PREDICAMENT

We have lost our story. This is how Thomas Berry describes our predicament.[2] This is why the assumptions of our society are no longer working, and why our individual picture of reality does not seem to coincide with what appears to be going on around us. As Miriam Therese MacGillis has suggested, we have no road map, no ethic to pass on.[3]

In many ways we are like the children whose old-maid aunt loved jigsaw puzzles. Each Christmas the kindly woman would give her nieces and nephews two elaborate puzzles. The boys and girls would thank their aunt dutifully and tell her just how much they appreciated and enjoyed the gifts. The children were stretching the truth a bit. They did admire the pictures on the boxes, but they really never bothered to put a puzzle together. Then, one rainy day when they had nothing better to do, they decided to assemble one of the scores of jigsaws now stashed away in their closets. After trying unsuccessfully for a long time, they discovered their aunt's joke — she had switched puzzle boxes. The myriad pieces on the table before them did not correspond to the picture they were trying to assemble.

In many ways we are like the Burmese peasants I once heard British economist E. F. Schumacher describe.[4] In the village economies that still existed in Burma shortly after World War II, the peasants could obtain almost everything they needed without money. They had not yet been imprisoned by the Western delusions of "progress." The British, however, sought to aid the country by bringing it into the fold of the industrial age. Factories were constructed, and villagers were soon walking from their homes to work in the newly established companies. They seemed to enjoy strolling together over the rough roads, but the factory managers thought that this was too inefficient. It wasted too much time. To alleviate the problem, the corporate men offered to create a horse-drawn trolley service. The peasants were surveyed to find out if they would ride the trolley. Yes, they responded, it sounded like fun, and the price was okay.

But during the first week of service, not one person boarded the trolley; they all turned and looked the other way as it approached. The driver would whip the horse as he came by, urging the poor animal over the steep terrain. When surveyed again to find out why no one took advantage of the new convenience, everyone gave the same answer: "Who would ride that trolley? Look at how the driver treats the horse!"

The peasants' circle of compassion still embraced all living creation. They did not experience themselves as separate from the horse, or removed from the whole of nature and its beauty. Schumacher decided that these people enjoyed a freedom that he would never know. A dozen years later he returned to Burma. By now diesel buses had replaced the horse-drawn trolley. Crowded with people, they sped through villages, spewing fumes and dust over the countryside, scattering chickens, and occasionally killing a goat that had not yet adapted to the idea of progress. The peasants, Schumacher realized, were now imprisoned too.

AN OPTICAL DELUSION

The picture on the puzzle of reality given to me by my formal education does not fit the reality I now affirm. As a college professor, I passed on to my students the same portrait of progress that the British imposed on the Burmese peasants, the same optical delusion of consciousness. It resembled a tinker toy set. It was a model suggested over four centuries ago by such classical scientists as Sir Isaac Newton and Francis Bacon, a worldview that eventually opened the door to the development of modern technology. The Earth and the universe were compared to a great machine. Newton lived in a clockwork cosmos. Bacon's empirical method was regarded as the most adequate means for identifying all of the pieces in the grand puzzle, and when humans came to understand how all of these worked, they would be in charge of the machine, in charge of Earth. If a part broke, the experts could fix it, or simply replace it. They could even redesign the machine to their own liking if they so desired.

I later learned in kindergarten that the mechanistic model of reality is "the old manner of thinking," an approach that appeared at first to liberate, but now serves to imprison. It puts great power into the hands of humans, allowing men and women to probe the bowels of their machine, to pry into its innermost recesses in ways never before thought possible. In the classical view of the cosmos, thanks to the musings of René Descartes, consciousness is understood as residing in humans only. Since the Scientific Revolution, Earth and her nonhuman inhabitants, her vegetation, mountains, rivers and seas have lost their numinous quality. They have been regarded as mere mechanical manifestations, resources to be exploited rather than sources of intrinsic value. But it has not always been so.

Earlier models of reality considered all of creation to possess a kind of consciousness — the world was regarded as sacred. In the ancient world, humans were seen as inseparable from nature, one with the universe. All creatures, including humans, lived enmeshed in a mysterious web of being. Each had value, each had a purpose, and thus a right to exist. A nonphysical reality pervaded the cosmos. The world had a soul.[5]

As a child, I experienced, as many children do, nature's mysterious web. I believed I could communicate with trees. I made the acquaintance of animals with whom I shared my thoughts. I assumed more was going on in the world than anyone talked about. But as I grew older doubts began to cloud my heart and mind. Was this perception merely my imagination? Perhaps society's "soundtrack" is really all there is. *Human* society. *Human* history. No mystery. Just business-as-usual. *Human* business.

If there *were* anything else, I began to think, we would certainly know about it. If there were a better way to perceive reality, then the men in the white lab coats would certainly tell us. But some scientists had been telling us. Early in the twentieth century, men like Einstein, Heisenberg, and Bîhr, opened our eyes to the fact that much more was going on in our world than we could imagine, more than their finely tuned instruments could adequately measure. It would be another half century before the general public would hear and understand that there was an alternative way to think about reality. Unfortunately, I was not one of those listening.

At the time I enrolled in graduate school, no one told me about Einstein's prison, or that I was suffering from an "optical delusion of consciousness." No one mentioned that what I should be about in my education is widening my circle of compassion, thinking in a new manner, embracing all of creation in its beauty. These lessons would have to wait until kindergarten.

WE ARE IGNORANT

The greatest discovery of modern science is that humans are ignorant. According to Lewis Thomas, this realization may be the saving grace of the twentieth century and beyond.[6] If taken to heart, it could result in a kinder, friendlier human presence on planet Earth. If three-year-old Aubrey Elizabeth can fish this understanding out of the electronic sea, she will master Einstein's new manner of thinking. But it will not be a return to the superstitions that preceded the Scientific Revolution, nor will it be the mechanistic way of thinking so characteristic of the modern era. Science will remain, but mystery will return. Paradox and logic will not be at odds; they will complement each other.

I am hopeful that Aubrey Elizabeth's future will not be one of catastrophe. She and my other grandchildren (Layla, Kenyon, Matthew, Christopher, and Summer Skye) will participate in the next step of discovery. They will widen their circle of compassion, embrace all living creation and the whole of nature in its beauty. My hope comes from the lessons I learned in kindergarten. I try in this book to pass on the gift of hope given to me by my teachers:

- A 70-year-old Florida woman (one of several ecologically disposed "Grandmothers" I once knew) who was hopelessly in love with the creatures that inhabited the stream behind her house, the weeds in her yard, the trees overhead, and the students she taught.

- A Dominican nun from New Jersey whose life of contentment collapsed when she suddenly realized how little she knew about the world in which she lived. When her prison doors swung open, she left the life of an art teacher to learn the art of sacred agriculture.

• A 14-year-old boy, "Ben," whom I saw only once. He asked me two questions which began a journey that continues as I write these words. The imaginary conversations I have had with him over the last few years are recorded in italics throughout these pages.

COSMIC AMPHIBIAN

Someday my grandchildren will pull down a window in their computer and click their mouse on the term "cosmic amphibian." The following information will flash on their screen. If it doesn't, it should:

• The Earth spins around her axis at the speed of 1,000 miles an hour at the equator. One revolution takes 23 hours, 56 minutes and 4.1 seconds. But as we spin we are also on another circular journey: we orbit our daystar, the sun. Traveling at the speed of 66,600 miles an hour, this second journey takes 365 days, 6 hours, 9 minutes and 9.54 seconds to complete. In the annual pilgrimage around this great star we travel 595,000,000 miles.

• The planet's 24-hour circular journey, while one continuous movement, is divided into day and night, just as each of us, though one reality, is a twofold mystery of body and spirit. These are not separate realities but one mingled mystery which makes each pilgrim a "cosmic amphibian." As such we experience both an interior and exterior life.

To know only one aspect of existence makes the space traveler incomplete.

• The Earth and the companion planets that circle the sun as a family are also moving a million miles a day outward into space. None of us travels home alone. Together with our companion pilgrims, with the entire solar family and other sun colonies of the universe, we are involved in a cosmic dance which is a corporate mystical quest.[7]

What follows is the story of the inward and outward journey of one cosmic amphibian, one who seeks and welcomes all companion pilgrims.

NOTES

1. Albert Einstein, as quoted in the Foundation for Global Community journal *Timeline* no. 24 (Nov./Dec. 1995): 24.

2. See, for example, Berry's inspirational book, *The Dream of the Earth* (San Francisco: Sierra Club Books, 1988), and a more recent text co-authored with Brian Swimme, *The Universe Story: From the Primordial Flaring Forth to the Ecozoic Era* (San Francisco: HarperSanFrancisco, 1992).

3. Miriam Therese MacGillis, "Fate of the Earth," audiotape available from Global Perspectives, P.O. Box 925, Sonoma, CA 95476.

4. For an excellent introduction to Schumacher's work and thought, see his now classic text *Small Is Beautiful: Economics as if People Mattered* (New York: Harper & Row, 1973).

5. Two excellent resources on the demise of the organic model of the cosmos at the hands of the Scientific Revolution are Carolyn Merchant, *The Death of Nature: Women, Ecology, and the Scientific Revolution* (New York: Harper & Row, 1980); and Stephen Toulmin, *The Return to Cosmology: Postmodern Science and the Theology of Nature* (Berkeley: University of California Press, 1982). Alfred North Whitehead also provides a penetrating philosophical analysis of the development of science up to the twentieth century in *Science and the Modern World* (New York: The Free Press, 1953; originally published in 1925).

6. Lewis Thomas has been instrumental in the popularization of scientific research that, without his very readable explications, would remain lost to the general public. See, for example, his book, *Lives of a Cell* (New York: Viking, 1974). See also Timothy Ferris, *Coming of Age in the Milky Way* (New York: William Morrow, 1988) 328, the source for this reference.

7. See Edward Hays's, *Prayers for a Planetary Pilgrim* (Leavenworth, KS: Forest of Peace Books, 1979) for a story about cosmic amphibians.

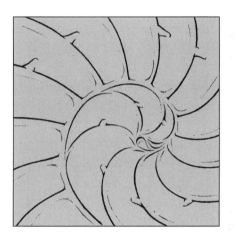

Life altered the atmosphere and gentled the sunlight. It turned the naked rocks of the continents into friable soil and clothed them with a richly variegated mantle of green which captured the energy of our own star for the use of living things on Earth, and it softened the force of the winds.... Working with amazing strength and endurance, life transformed an ugly and barren landscape into a benign and beautiful place where wildflowers carpet the hillsides and birds embroider the air with song. The story of how all this came to pass is a shining example of the creative forces working within nature.

Louise Young
The Unfinished Universe[1]

1

A 100-MILLION-YEAR BUSINESS REPORT

Helen's living room was full, but there was nothing unusual about that. Couches and chairs were pulled into a circle and the women took their places. One sat on the floor, legs crossed, back straight. The meeting began much like any other but concluded on a rather serious note: a vow was made, one that would change the lives of all of those present. Two years later, the vow changed my life, for by that time the Council of Grandmothers had completed their proposed 100-Million-Year Business Report for Planet Earth. When I was invited to review the project, I was unprepared for the gift that I would receive from these women... and from a fourteen-year-old boy. This chapter is my attempt to pass on their gift. As I write this book, I imagine the boy looking over my shoulder, questioning, counseling.

THE COUNCIL OF GRANDMOTHERS

The Council of Grandmothers began as a book group for senior citizens, but it soon exploded. A woman in love ignited the fuse. Helen Wallace was in love with her students, in love with the friends who crowded into her house and into her life, in love with the coots, ducks, turtles, fish, hummingbirds, beetles, orchids, grass, even the weeds that inhabited her backyard and an adjoining canal.

For twenty years Helen and I were colleagues at Miami-Dade Community College. She was the kind of woman who often rushed into faculty meetings breathless. It was no different when meeting with friends or with a church committee. Usually she was excited about something she had just discovered: a new way to think, a new manner of teaching or feeling, always something beautiful. Out of the blue, she would light a candle, tell us to close our eyes, and explain how Native Americans loved the land, how they treated it with respect and considered all creatures on Earth to be members of their family. Helen believed that the most important lesson we could teach our students was to love and respect the planet. She believed in tough love, calling a spade a spade, keeping one's vows no matter what.

Helen's best friend was Sally Milledge, also a member of the book group. Sally described for me the study that led to the explosion.

"We had read a book about Albert Einstein," she said, "about the worries that plagued him in his old age. There was also a book about Native Americans, especially the Iroquois Federation of Six Nations. The Federation was the first large scale democracy we know about. It inspired Benjamin Franklin and the founders of our constitution. Yet, it wasn't given credit in our history books. We wondered why."

The Iroquois called North America "Turtle Island." When Columbus discovered Turtle Island, the indigenous peoples were governing themselves. Many had instituted systems of checks and balances. Clans, tribes, and nations did not want their chiefs to have the final say on matters of grave importance. Chiefs were usually male, but not always. There were great warriors and powerful medicine men, but for real wisdom, the people turned to the grandmothers, to the Council of Grandmothers.

THE SEVENTH GENERATION TEST

The Council reviewed decisions made by the chiefs. The old women sat in a circle and applied what they called "the Seventh Generation Test." They did not debate. They sat in silence and pondered the issue presented to them. Their question was simple: "How will the decisions made by our chief affect our children seven generations into the future?"

The answer didn't come from the head, for wisdom resides in the heart. The Grandmothers knew that the answer was not a possession of one person, but of all in the circle. It spanned time and space and came from the memories of the ancestors. The decision might take a few minutes or many hours to make, but when the women rose, all had agreed. Their judgment was final.

"We asked ourselves," Sally said, "'How many decisions of our chiefs today — chiefs of government, business, education, religion — would pass the Seventh Generation Test? We all agreed that very few would."

Why would so few decisions of our contemporary chiefs pass the Seventh Generation Test? Why are so many rational human beings today so out of touch with the reality of life, with the reality of their children's future?

3

The women kept coming back to Einstein's warning: humans must master a "new manner of thinking" or drift into "ultimate catastrophe." Ultimate catastrophe — this was the heritage that they were leaving their grandchildren. Sally recalled the explosion that followed.

"Helen announced that she had *had* it with official explanations. Enough was enough. Why should our grandchildren have to inherit *our* debts, *our* trash, *our* poisons, and the consequences of *our* blindness and greed?"

That afternoon Helen reconstituted the Council of Grandmothers. She lit a candle and a dozen grandmothers made a vow. They would, at least, find out why humans had gotten so far off track, why our intelligent species — *Homo sapiens,* "wise hominids" — was bankrupting our planet.

The bankruptcy idea stuck. Sally suggested that they create a business report for Earth, a profit and loss statement for the planet. It would be a kind of end-of-the-year graph like the ones General Motors or IBM include in their stockholders' reports, something the male chiefs would understand. Sally understood business. Statistics, too.

One hundred million years seemed about right — just enough time to see the big picture, and to see where humans fit in. The women wanted to offer their grandchildren a model of reality that made sense, something the next generation could believe in. If at all possible, the Grandmothers wanted to leave something that would give the next generations a reason for hope.

The Council met every week for two years. They formed study teams, took college courses, went to conferences, read books. At the meetings, Helen would light a candle as the women sat silently in a circle, then each Grandmother would make a report. When they concluded, each woman would hurry back into the "unreal world" to gather more information. Their most pressing questions: how successful was Earth's business one hundred million years ago? Seventy five? Fifty? Twenty five? One million years ago? They scavenged cardboard boxes from supermarkets and filled them with charts, articles, books, and, of course, their own written reports.

THE BIG PICTURE

By the time they came to me, the big picture was beginning to emerge. They were ready to compile their 100-Million-Year Business Report for Planet Earth. Helen and Sally asked if I would meet with them for half a day once a week for eight weeks. We would convene at the Environmental Center I was directing at the time, their hope being that I could critique the picture of reality that they had arrived at. I agreed to help as best I could.

Each week the elderly women carried the heavy boxes, two to a side, into the pine woods that surrounded the Center (lugging boxes wasn't my job, they said). We had to meet outside because there was not room enough indoors for the 100-million-year graph they were going to display. Sally held up a carpenter's chalk line that she had just purchased from a local hardware store. The string, when extended, was 100 feet long.

Silently, the women formed a circle. Some sat on boxes, others lowered themselves onto a fallen log, or helped each other sink to the cushion of pine needles on the ground. Helen placed a stubby white candle into a red clay bowl filled with sand and lit it with a tiny gas torch. She sat shielding the flame from the breeze. Silence. And more silence. Maybe fifteen minutes altogether. I thought I was wasting the morning. What had I gotten myself into? A vague uneasiness began to grow within me. I sucked resin from a pine needle, listened to a redheaded woodpecker chip away at a tree, watched a centipede zigzag over the bluejean pant leg of a grandmother nearby. I let my thoughts race. I was unaware of it then, but I was embarking on a journey that would change my manner of thinking irrevocably. It would transform my idea of what it means to be a member of my species, an inhabitant of the earth, a teacher, an environmentalist, a husband, a father. It would especially change my view of what it means to be a grandfather.

In the first meeting I was lost in the chaos of my thoughts, but then the silence ended. Sally stood up and extended the chalk line to its full length. The one-hundred-foot string represented one hundred million years. Sally informed us that we were going to consider the success of Earth's business along every foot of the string. It occurred to me that I still did not know what we were measuring. What *is* Earth's business?

I asked Sally. The women looked at me, incredulous. This was the expert who was going to critique their model? Sally extended her hand. I stood up and she led me, as if I were in kindergarten, to where she had tied the far end of the string to a low hanging branch. Out of hearing, away from the others, she admonished me.

"Mac, I assumed you knew. Earth's business is life."

I was in kindergarten.

BACK TO KINDERGARTEN

Most of the information contained in their boxes was old stuff to me. Unpacking their files each week, they uncovered more and more pieces of a puzzle. The pieces were familiar, but the way they were finally assembled into the big picture was a revelation. Their depiction of reality intrigued and appalled me. I both embraced and fought it.

In the times of silence, I realized my real need for kindergarten lessons. Einstein was right: I needed to master a new manner of thinking, a new way of knowing — heart-knowing instead of head-thinking. The candle communicated at a level that I was only beginning to grasp. It was like a flickering Morse code, gathering data from a level deep within each of us, a depth that we moderns take pride in ignoring. It dawned on me that without these times of silent meditation in the circle, the Grandmothers could not have put the puzzle together the way they did.

The picture they assembled was as beautiful as it was simple. A scientist friend told me their 100-million-year graph was, indeed, scientifically elegant. Then again, another told me it was sheer fantasy, that it had nothing to do with real science. I do not believe that the work of the Grandmothers can be so easily categorized. I did not know then that scientists, philosophers, and theologians were constructing similar models of reality, models that would challenge my old ways of perceiving the world. Interestingly, their models were not too far removed from the organic worldviews of a variety of ancient peoples: Turtle Islanders, Greeks, Egyptians, Mayans, Mesopotamians, Africans, Chinese, East Indians, Tibetans, Eskimos. The list is long.

A MANAGEMENT SYSTEM

Sally informed me of the purpose of Earth's business report. It was to measure the planet's ongoing capacity to support life. Every species in this scheme was conceived as a business of sorts, each making "investments" in the future. From time to time, Earth's business climate changed. The ventures that were no longer profitable abruptly disappeared.

"We think we know how Earth's management system works," Sally said. "At every point on the graph, we see the results of three management functions. Each function depends on feedback loops, like those in a computer program, except in this case the feedback loops are infinite. There are no edges, no distinct divisions between one function and another. Yet, the effect of each function is always discernible. Earth's management system is embedded in everything."

The women tied colored ribbons to the string to mark points at which there were significant breakthroughs. These were times of crisis in the business of life on Earth, and each prepared the soil for change. At each red ribbon the women showed how the three functions of Earth's management system were evident.

- *First function*: The Grandmothers called the first function *diversification*. Everywhere, at all times, Earth could be seen diversifying its investments. Just like an international conglomerate, Earth seeks new business opportunities in every environmental niche. The planet's creativity seems unlimited. It responds to every new possibility, no matter how remote or insignificant it may seem.

- *Second Function: Relatedness.* There are no loners, no islands in the system. No life enterprise is ever isolated from the whole. What looks like a chaotic struggle for survival is, in fact, the tip of an iceberg of incredible order. Every enterprise is part of a network of related networks, of food chains and energy exchanges. Because of these relationships, every species, every enterprise, turns a profit, i.e., puts back into the system a little more than it takes out. As a result, topsoil accumulates, Earth's chemistry becomes more stable, fossil energy is stored underground. Business relationships become more complex and life's potential increases as one moves further along the string.

- *Third Function: Purposefulness.* Earth's management system has never been random; it has always been going somewhere. Its feedback loops not only assure the profitability of Earth's businesses, but move Earth steadily toward some yet indiscernible destiny. There is a design in Earth's automatic management system.

"A design?" I objected. "That is an anthropomorphic concept." The women were assigning human attributes to nature. I told them that this was not at all scientific.
"What *is* scientific?" They pinned me down. I explained the scientific method, which they knew. "Replication is the key," I said. "When an experiment can be replicated then you can call it objective — not subjective, and certainly not anthropomorphic." Helen said that she thought nature was scientific. It conducts wonderful experiments, replicates them time after time, then im-

proves on them. Maybe our anthropomorphic species is an experiment. Humans are not immune to the effects of Earth's management system, she explained. We are merely part of its diversification and relatedness. We couldn't separate ourselves from the planet's feedback loops if we tried.

"We are part of the design," she said. "If two years of study has taught us anything, it's that. I don't think humankind is a mistake, but it's a possibility. We haven't figured out our purpose yet."

I said nothing. I didn't know enough to agree or disagree. I was still in kindergarten, but I was beginning to learn.

THE 100-FOOT GRAPH

For weeks I watched as the Grandmothers transferred data from their boxes to their one-hundred-foot string graph. For the most part, their sources were impeccable: energy flow charts from Dr. Howard Odum at the University of Florida; statistics from Dr. Ross McCluney at the Florida Solar Energy Center; United Nations' graphs showing energy consumption, resource use, population impact, the human impact from the time of early hunter-gatherers to modern industrialized civilization.

Sixty-five feet back on the string, the Grandmothers hung an extra large red ribbon — a major breakthrough. Sixty-five million years ago, a host of new possibilities for life businesses opened up. One theory is that a massive meteorite struck Earth somewhere near Central America. The collision caused a worldwide cloud of dust, water, and smoke. The planet's climate underwent a monumental transformation.

Until this event, dinosaurs had been profitable on the planet for a period of about 150 million years. Now they were phased out by Earth's automatic management system. Sea turtles, which had existed just as long, were somehow able to weather the storm. They continued to serve a purpose, to put back more than they took out. But more than half of Earth's life businesses disappeared. The Grandmothers speculated that Earth's capacity to support life would decrease at this juncture.

It didn't. Instead, innumerable new niches for business opened up. Marginal species that had not really amounted to much in the past now suddenly blossomed. One group that profited from the change in climate was mammals. These ratty creatures had up until now been insignificant members of the Earth community, but with new opportunities everywhere, they took off in a frenzy of diversification. Other winners in what looked like a catastrophe were flowering plants like the seed-bearing ancestors of corn, wheat, rice and other cereals. Earth was on its way to becoming a garden paradise.

During our sixth session, the Grandmothers completed their graph. On it they identified two recent breakthroughs, both more portentous than what had occurred 65 million years ago. One reached about a million years into our past, the other, they calculated, took place in the last half of the nineteenth century. These two changes, they said, were the most significant events in the history of life on Earth. Business would never be the same. I had to agree.

Each change effected a radical discontinuity with the past. Each was an historical turning point — historical in that life on Earth moved into a new reality. The name of the game changed. These two events, the Grandmothers said, should be the starting points of all human education, yet they are ignored. Without familiarity with these two watersheds in Earth's story, the study of history, natural science, social science, philosophy, and religion only leads students down a blind alley. Helen quoted R. Buckminster Fuller:

> Education hooks us on a game of life that has nothing to do with the way the universe is going.[2]

"It hooks us," Helen said, "because we don't know our species' history, and we don't know where *we* are going."

I objected to Fuller's language. Fuller was a good scientist, I said, but science cannot prove that the universe is going anywhere. By making such a statement, Fuller had attributed human characteristics to the natural world. Helen's rebuttal was simple: humans are part of the natural world. She reminded me that our attributes are merely a gift from the universe.

The gift was granted about a million years ago when our species was cut free from Earth's automatic management system. This was the first recent breakthrough referred to above. This event required billions of years of preparation. The human characteristics of freedom and self-consciousness made possible new kinds of diversification, new kinds of relatedness. Unlocked from the dictates of instinct, human creativity could now transform the planet. Diverse cultures, music, art, religion, science and architecture would eventually blossom. Only humans were free to create and destroy at will; destroy one ecosystem, move on to destroy another. Only humans could ignore the functions of Earth's management system with seeming impunity.

But the illusion of impunity ended a little over a century ago with the advent of the Industrial Revolution of the mid-nineteenth century, the second portentous watershed. Now, for the first time, our species achieved the power to consume faster than the other life businesses on Earth could produce. It was an historic event; the Grandmothers marked it with a red ribbon. For nearly a hundred feet the string rose steadily reflecting the diversification, the fecundity, of the business of life on Earth, but with this new ribbon the continuity of the graph was disrupted. Earth's capacity to support life was, at last, on the decline.

"Girls, there'll be a curve," Sally said.

We were all assembled beneath an old, gnarled pine. I looked at its weathered trunk, then at the group of weathered grandparents. I felt a kinship with the tree. On one branch a mockingbird trilled an aria and we all smiled. I felt a kinship with the bird, too. Sally traced in the air the possible courses the string might now follow. Her question: how severely should we represent the decline? How rapidly was Earth's capacity to support life diminishing?

"I'll do some calculations," she said. "I'll tell you next week."

A SHOCKING REVELATION

At our next meeting we gathered again under the gnarled pine. The same mockingbird was singing. There was more breeze than usual coming from the Everglades, so Helen's candle blazed and sputtered alternately through the initial silence. In retrospect, the rough weather was apropos to the occasion, for it was on this morning that I received my harshest kindergarten lesson.

As our quiet meditation ended, Sally stood up and looked at each of us lounging in our ragged circle. We waited for her report.

"Girls," she said, "I've got news for you."

She held up the loose end of the string and let it drop. "There is no curve. The line goes almost straight down."

I was afraid that this might be the case, but I was unprepared for the feelings that soon began to overwhelm me.

"Girls, do you know what this means? It means...." Sally spread her arms out in front of her and made a sucking sound. "It means that in 150 years humans have sucked up a hundred million years' worth of Earth's productivity! One species is consuming the planet, and consuming it faster every year!"

Sally pointed to where her end of the string hung limp. The line plummeted to a point level with where the string began its gradual incline 100 feet away. I felt my stomach cramp. I didn't say anything, but I must have turned pale. Only once had I experienced anything like this, when a doctor phoned me long distance while I was on vacation and told me that my heart had failed the stress test I had taken before leaving. "Do nothing strenuous," he warned, "until you can get yourself to a hospital for a another test." I was able to get my heart under control, but this seemed out of my control.

If the graph were in fact accurate, then modern civilization as we know it rests on an illusory foundation. Over the past several centuries, history and science have colluded to create a make-believe world. To move on from here, we would have to reconstruct this model of the cosmos, take it apart piece by piece, and then learn to live in accordance with Earth's management system and design. That would be a job for tough love. I couldn't understand the women's reaction... or, rather, lack of reaction. Why weren't they feeling the same shock of despair? I knew there were inconsistencies in the graph, that Sally's assumptions were not all precise, but I believed the picture it portrayed was tragically close to reality.

I lowered my head between my knees. When I looked up I saw the Grandmothers staring at me.

"Mac, what's wrong?" Helen said. "You look sick."

"What do you mean, 'What's wrong?' You've proved your point. We're bankrupting the Earth."

"Maybe, but we don't know that yet. This is what we've been looking for, a model we can believe in. Now we will look for what it means."

I told her I didn't get it. She explained that the group had some time ago chosen four scientists whose opinions they could trust: R. Buckminster Fuller, Scottish ecologist Ian McHarg, British scientist Jacob Bronowski, and astronomy whiz Carl Sagan. At major breakthroughs on the graph, a team of Grandmothers would work with the ideas of each of these men. They would ask how Buck (or Ian, or Jacob, or Carl) would interpret the breakthrough. After two years of study, they were on a first-name basis with their famous mentors. The four teams, Helen announced, would give their final report at our eighth session. They would then decide what the last watershed on the graph really means.

UNEXPECTED VISITORS

I reserved the Center's meeting room for the final session of the Council of Grandmothers. We moved indoors, or almost. The walls of the room folded up and out to let in the breeze. Outside we could see the pines and hear the music of the mockingbirds. We also noticed a teacher and five boys touring the grounds. Helen transferred the red ribbon breakthroughs from the string to a blackboard. My job was to review the graph, then the four teams of Grandmothers would give their report on its meaning. Just before I began, I saw the teacher herd the boys into our room. Sally whispered to me that they were from a local middle school, 14-year-olds. Their teacher wanted them to listen.

The boys seemed not to like the idea; they looked bored. I almost fell for it, almost made the biggest mistake of my teaching career. I knew I could entertain them with a box of photovoltaic experiments in the closet. We could all go outside in the sun and the boys could solder their own solar engines. They'd go back to whatever school they came from with a good report, and other teachers and students would come.

But I didn't do it. I still don't know why. As soon as I started talking about the graph, I was glad I hadn't switched our agenda. The boys seemed to come alive. They seemed to understand what we were doing much better than we did. They were computer experts, of course, and the feedback loops that kept Earth's businesses profitable fascinated them.

About half way through the session, something began to happen that I still cannot get a handle on. In a strange kind of way, the boys seemed to be teaching us. They hardly said a word, but there was a flow of energy that we had not experienced before. I was caught up in the drama of the business report as I covered the blackboard with a maze of symbols and lines. Earth's business investments were continually diversifying, its life-support networks were becoming more complex, the management system was going somewhere. When I arrived at the last breakthrough, I slashed a vertical chalk line down the center of the board.

The picture was clear. For the first time ever, one species had achieved the power to consume faster than the Earth could produce. The boys stared at the graph fascinated, eyes bright. The historic reality seemed more than obvious to them. But it didn't fit into the picture of reality they were learning at school, or anywhere else for that matter.

FOUR SCIENTISTS REPORT

We took a bathroom break. The boys were back in their seats first as the four teams of Grandmothers organized the last details of their reports. When the women were ready, each interpreted the graph from the perspective of her favorite scientist. They didn't do it the way I would have, with a chart or an outline of main points leading to a logical conclusion. They had studied videos of their mentors, had observed each man's personality, the way he walked and talked. They were well-versed in every nuance of their master's demeanor and were ready to become that man. They acted out what Bucky might say to this distinguished group, or Ian, Jacob, or Carl.

R. BUCKMINSTER FULLER[3]

The representative for team one came out of her chair like a boxer dancing into the ring... an ancient boxer, that is: R. Buckminster Fuller is 85. She had studied Fuller's three-hour, nonstop lectures on video. She imitated perfectly his bent posture, his bouncy gate and rapid-fire talk.

"Ladies," she barked, "you've done a good job."

She pranced in front of the blackboard pointing to each breakthrough on the graph.

"See, there. It's been a long relay race. You've pictured each lap perfectly. Now, look where the line starts down. You know what that means, don't you? It's the last lap. The last lap in a race that began four billion years ago.

"Do you know what that means?" She paused, waiting. "The last lap is the final exam, a final exam to determine whether humans qualify to continue on this planet, qualify to go on to the next race."

Silence filled the room. We heard hammering outside. In the woods mockingbirds were ganging up on a crow. The bent, prancing grandmother straightened.

"That gives me hope," she said. "We've passed exams before. We can pass this one, too."

IAN MCHARG[4]

Team two's representative had the face of a thunderhead. The oldest, toughest, most gnarled grandmother was Ian McHarg. She never unfolded her arms as she surveyed the graph.

"Bah," she snorted, "The last thing we need now is R. Buckminster Fuller's romanticism. You girls have done a good job, but let's at least be honest, call a spade a spade. I'll tell you what you're looking at. A medical chart. A medical chart of a wonderful, healthy, robust organism. And what's happened?" She glared at where the line turned down, the part of the graph that reflected human consumption of 100 million years of Earth's productivity. "One cell in that organism has become a what?" She let us squirm. One of the boys whispered, "A cancer?"

"Yes, a cancer that is multiplying and consuming everything. The human cancer will go on consuming until what? Until the Earth dies?"

Silence.

"Not to worry," the gnarled one said, "Earth's climate will change, and when it can no longer support that cancerous cell, Earth will blossom again."

She let herself go limp and sank to a full lotus position on the floor. "McHarg," she said, "doesn't give me any hope."

JACOB BRONOWSKI[5]

Another grandmother made her way to the front of the room, smiling benignly at both "Buck" and "Ian". The smile was unmistakable. She was Jacob Bronowski, a man who could see many sides to every question. The woman transformed herself into the courtly British scientist.

"Yes," she mused, "Fuller has a good point. Girls, I'd say you've charted each lap in the relay race rather nicely. But McHarg has a good point, too. Your graph does have the appearance of a medical chart. You show Earth's good health as a living organism."

Unhurriedly, she traced the long upward climb of the graph on the blackboard. Her finger stopped where the line plunged down.

"What's this? Ah, I'll tell you what you've shown here. The human species has begun an irreversible mutation. What is a mutation? A species that's changed in some fundamental way. You show lots of them on your 100-million-year chart. As you know, some mutations become cancers. If humankind becomes a cancer, then McHarg is right. But other mutations become better fitting species. If humans adapt well, then Fuller is right. In my opinion, it's too early to tell which we will become."

The grandmother's gentlemanly composure faded.

"I think that's what we've been doing these two years," she said. "Giving birth to a better fitting species. That gives me hope."

CARL SAGAN[6]

Team four's representative stood boyishly in the middle of the room. Carl Sagan exuded optimism. The youngest grandmother pointed at the graph on the blackboard.

"How parochial!" she announced. "Sure, ladies, you've pinpointed a turning point in life on Earth. But look...."

She pointed to a satellite photograph of Earth on one wall.

"That is a beautiful planet. But there are a billion galaxies with trillions of suns. As a mathematician and an astronomer, I say there is no way to calculate the number of planets where life might be seeded in the universe. Now, I'll tell you what your graph shows, and shows beautifully. Wherever life is seeded anywhere in the universe, it will go through three stages."

Suddenly, she threw a handful of sunflower seeds across the room. The boys were so caught up in her performance they applauded.

"Wherever life is seeded in the universe, it will eventually achieve intelligence. See, you've shown that first stage. In the second stage, intelligent life learns to use technology — the lever, the wheel, the automobile, the bulldozer, the jet plane, the nuclear bomb. The third stage arrives when that intelligent life develops a technology powerful enough to... powerful enough to do what?"

"To destroy itself!" the boys chorused.

"Exactly. Intelligent life on a planet called Earth has achieved the third stage. Now, I have a question. When intelligent life anywhere in the universe develops a technology powerful enough to destroy itself, will it? Will it destroy itself?"

She stood silent, letting the question sink in. The Grandmothers were all religious: Jews, Christians, the woman on the floor was a Buddhist. The young grandmother then did what Sagan probably would have done. She stepped sideways and announced:

"I am an atheist. Here's what I think. Yes, an intelligent species will destroy itself, unless that intelligent species is guided by some higher purpose."

Smiling, the young Grandmother returned to her seat.

FROM DESPAIR TO EXCITEMENT

Helen nudged me and I stood up. I was supposed to lead a discussion about the four perspectives. I never did. Before I could begin, one of the boys came up out of his chair and walked slowly to where I stood. I moved out of his way as he proceeded on to the blackboard.

I can see him now as clearly as I saw him that day years ago, a perplexed look on his face, head shaking, finger pointing at the graph. I remember his exact words.

"Who would want to live there...," he pointed to where the line on the graph was rising steadily, where Earth's management system worked perfectly, "...if they could live here?" He pointed to where the line plunged straight down.

We adults looked at each other confused. We had thought the boys were with us, but maybe they had missed the point. Then, slowly, it dawned on us: the boy understood much more than we did. Everything presented that day had come together in his brain. Two years of work by the Grandmothers was synthesized, or mutated.

He was at the board for only a few minutes, but in that brief period of time the Grandmothers found what they wanted most: a model of reality with hope for their grandchildren. The boy saw the graph at a level I had missed. He shared enough to change my response from despair to excitement. It was clear to us that he understood three things.

First, he realized that the 100-million-year period shown on the graph -- and billions of years before that - were all preparation for now, for this moment of the final exam, this time of mutation and change. Who would want to live in the time of preparation, no matter how good it may have been, if one could live in the time for which everything was being prepared? Second, he understood that the downward plunge toward bankruptcy was necessary, even essential. This is the lesson that many spiritual traditions have tried to teach us from the beginning, that humans slumber in the illusion of self-sufficiency, believing themselves capable of taking over each of nature's three management functions. When they realize their mistake, however, they may then move on to realize the limits of their intellectual endeavors, and that the final exam is more a test of the heart than of the head.

Third, he understood that he was "it," that if this mutation were going to take place, it would have to take place in him. The decision whether humans will become a cancer or a better fitting species will be made in individual human beings. It will not be made in places of power by politicians, not by religious leaders, teachers, or scientists. The decision will be made, if it is made at all, by grandparents, parents, and children who resolve that enough is enough, who practice the tough love of calling a spade a spade, who refuse to accept the excuses of our chiefs as to why our children must inherit our debts and our trash.

When the boy returned to his seat, I breathed a sigh of relief. My mind was on overload. As he started to sit, a thought seemed to hold him. He looked around the room and made eye contact with each of us. Then, waving an arm toward the board, he asked:

"If this is true, how come no one ever told us?"

He sat down. My first feeling was guilt.

"I couldn't have," I said, "I didn't know."

There was a long silence. He looked around the room and stopped when he came to me.

"Now that you know," he said, "what are you going to do about it?"

Now that *you* know, what are *you* going to do about it?

NOTES

1. Louise Young, *The Unfinished Universe* (New York: Simon & Schuster, 1986) 76.

2. R. Buckminster Fuller made this comment at a World Game workshop hosted by Miami-Dade Community College, and attended by Helen Wallace. The quote has also been printed on poster pictures of the 85 year-old Fuller as a kind of epigram for his life's work.

3. Resources for further study on the work of R. Buckminster Fuller include *A Blueprint for the Science and Culture of the Future* (New York: Macmillan, 1992), *Operating Manual or Spaceship Earth* (New York: Viking, 1991), and *R. Buckminster Fuller on Education* (Amherst: University of Massachusetts Press, 1979). Also, several outstanding audio tapes of Fuller's lectures are available from New Dimensions Foundation, P.O. Box 569, Ukiah, CA 95482-0569.

4. Resources for further study on the work of Ian McHarg include *A Quest for Life: An Autobiography* (New York: John Wiley & Sons, 1996), and *Design with Nature* (New York: Natural History Press, 1971).

5. Resources for further study on Jacob Bronowski's work include *Science and Human Values* (New York: HarperCollins, 1990), *The Origins of Knowledge and Imagination* (New Haven: Yale University Press, 1979), *The Common Sense of Science* (Cambridge: Harvard University Press, 1978), and *The Ascent of Man* (New York: Little, Brown & Co., 1976).

6. Resources for further study on the work of Carl Sagan include *Billions and Billions: Thoughts on Life and Death at the Brink of the Millennium* (New York: Random House, 1997), *Broca's Brain* (New York: Ballantine Books, 1986), *Cosmos* (New York: Ballantine Books, 1985), and *The Dragons of Eden* (New York: Ballantine Books, 1977).

If we compare the process of Earth's destruction (which is euphemistically termed "development") to the slow, patient evolution of myriad forms of life before and the global tragedies now unfolding and yet to come, we may get some sense of how the future will view us: not for the most part as the ingenious inventors of computers, spacecraft or biotechnological miracles, not as the great global culture of post modernism, nor as the purveyors of a high civilization of wealth and power, but as the people who for the sake of comfort and greed killed more than anyone else of what made this planet inhabitable, beautiful and (for those with eyes to see it) sacred. It is, therefore, no exaggeration to refer to our era as the Age of Devastation.

John Nolt
Down To Earth[1]

2

LOCKED IN THE ATTIC OF OURSELVES

The phone rang. It was Helen asking if I could please come to a meeting in her garage. The meeting was with Ben. She wanted to answer his questions and there was not much time.

"Ben who?" I asked.

"Our young benefactor. The boy who came to our last Council meeting. I gave him a name. How else could we talk to him?"

Ben. I liked it. The name seemed to fit. The Council of Grandmothers stored their files in Helen's garage and when I got there Helen was digging papers out of a cardboard box. Books were arranged on a table and she had taped a sheet of newsprint on one wall. Two chairs were squared off in front of each other where her car was usually parked. I caught a whiff of candle smoke.

Helen always over-prepared for everything, and there was no telling how long she had worked on this scene. She glanced at one chair and I sat. I knew she was planning a role play. She was a master at what she called "experiential education": learning not by "talking about," but by doing.

AN UNFINISHED DIALOGUE WITH BEN

"I'll be Ben," Helen said and motioned toward the chairs. We both sat down.

"Now, Dr. Smith," Helen slipped into her role, "can you answer my questions? Why didn't anyone ever tell us before? Now that you know, what are you going to do about it?"

I wasn't quite sure what to say.

"Take your time," she continued. "If we don't finish today, I'll come back tomorrow."

We didn't finish. During the next few months I would occasionally return to Helen's garage to continue our dialogue, and I was glad for the opportunity. But I could tell something was wrong. Once, Helen had trouble slipping in and out of her role. Only afterwards did I learn that my friend was suffering from the early stages of Alzheimer's.

On one visit Helen asked me to bring Sally, whose eyesight was failing. While driving to the garage, Sally told me that Helen's memory was not good, and to do the dialogues with me required great effort on her part. I thought then about Sally taking me by the hand and explaining her 100-foot string-graph, and Helen graciously allowing me to spout on about how anthropomorphic their business report was. It occurred to me that my kindergarten days with the "girls" would soon end.

And so they did — within six months Sally died. I was on leave from my job when Helen's daughters moved her to a nursing home in Michigan so she could be closer to her family. The house and garage were emptied and sold, the Council of Grandmothers disbanded. Now Helen, too, is dead.

DEAD BUT NOT GONE

Because Helen had been my teacher, I knew just what I needed to do when I read a most disturbing article in an issue of *Science News*. Though almost ten years had passed since that last day in Helen's garage, our dialogues were still fresh in my mind, and now I was compelled to revive them. I needed once again to role play with Ben.

By this time I had told the story of the boy and the 100-Million-Year Business Report many times in student seminars and workshops for teachers. It was here also that I helped to introduce a new kind of "literacy," a holistic approach to learning in which everything we study and experience is connected to everything else. It is interdisciplinary, "ecological," in the broadest sense of the term. It is called Earth Literacy, and at that time it was just beginning to be offered in a dozen Earth Literacy centers across the United States and in South America. The centers grew out of the work of a group called the Earth Literacy Communion.

We were a small, informal circle: three professors, a dean, a physicist, two free-lance workshop leaders, a physician, and three directors of retreat centers. We thought of ourselves less as a "network" than as a "communion," a term that seemed to reflect our mutual kindergarten status. Like my mentors of old, we would spend time in silence together. We celebrated Earth's creativity and tried to discover ways to mutate into a better fitting species on the planet. For my own purposes, The Earth Literacy Communion gave me the opportunity to carry on the work of the Council of Grandmothers, to respond to Ben's questions, and to pass on the gift that I had received some ten years earlier. Now the communion is assisting me in editing and publishing this book.[2]

A WOODEN SOCRATES

I began my imaginary dialogues by doing what I had seen Helen do: I role played Ben's part and mine. I got up and exchanged chairs, and imagined that I actually saw Ben sitting across from me. He was much older now, of course, perhaps in his mid-twenties. I could hear him talking clearly as I engaged in my conversation, but at another level, the discussion seemed real. Interestingly, I could not always predict what Ben would say next, for he seemed to know things that I did not know myself.

This reminded me of a story that Helen had told me once about mind researcher Jean Houston. As a child, Houston, the daughter of a script writer, had the opportunity to observe an impromptu backstage dialogue between ventriloquist Edgar Bergen and his dummy, Charlie McCarthy. As I spoke with Ben, I realized that what I was experiencing was the same peculiar phenomenon that Houston relates below:

Bergen was sitting with his back to us, talking to Charlie. We thought he was probably rehearsing, but as we listened we discovered that he was not rehearsing. He was asking Charlie ultimate questions, like", "Charlie, what is the nature of life?" "Charlie, what does it mean to be truly good?" "Charlie, what is love?" And this dummy, this little wooden being, was answering like a kind of wooden Socrates. The numinous knowings of millennia were pouring out his little wooden mouth. And Bergen would get so excited.

After a while my father got very skeptical and very worried, and so he coughed. Bergen turned around and saw us, turned beet red, and said, "Oh hello Jack, hi Jean, I see you caught us."

"Yes, Ed, what in the world are you doing?"

"Well, I'm talking to Charlie. He's the wisest person I know."

And my father said, "But Ed, that's your voice, that's your mind coming out of that dummy."

Ed said, "Yes, I suppose ultimately it is, but you know, when I ask him these questions and he answers me, I haven't the faintest idea of what he's going to say, and what he says astounds me with his wisdom, it is so much more than I know."

In my eight-year-old way, I knew then that what we are, compared to what we think we are, is so much vaster, that it's as if we are living in the attic of ourselves with the first, second, third and fourth floors relatively uninhabited and the basement locked, except when it explodes from time to time.[3]

Kindergarten with the Grandmothers had moved me out of the attic of my life, and my imaginary dialogues with Ben were now about to unlock my basement.

What follows is my first discussion with Ben in which my mentor, Helen, was not present to guide us, though she was certainly there in spirit. The subsequent chapters will also be addressed to our young benefactor, and from time to time I will slip into our imaginary dialogues (denoted by italics).

"That Feminine Touch"

In addition to arranging two chairs face to face, I had, as Helen would have wished, over-prepared for Ben's visit. I taped a sheet of newsprint on one wall. Across the top, I printed:

MALE SPERM COUNT PLUMMETS.

Below that was a question:

WHAT WILL BE THE ECONOMIC COST OF A GENERATION THAT CANNOT REPRODUCE ITSELF?

With masking tape, I attached a cardboard pocket (another of Helen's techniques) in which I placed several articles from some recent issues of *Science News*.

Ben sat in the chair opposite me, a young man with unmistakable curious eyes that took in every aspect of the room. He studied the newsprint I had taped on one wall.

"I think I know what the sperm count business is about," he said.

"You do?"

"Yes, I had mine counted. As a lark. A lot of us at the university did. We even got paid for it."

"What did you find out?"

"The lady in charge didn't tell us much. She said we were part of an important study. Gave us each our own count.

Can you imagine sending a woman to do research like that? We all just forgot about it as soon as we could."

"You didn't compare results. Doesn't that seem strange?"

"I thought about it later. At the time, it seemed too personal. She said we were all pretty low. About average for college students these days. I remember my count. Do you want to know what it was?"

"Let me guess."

"Go for it."

"I guess 65 to 70 million sperm per milliliter. How close did I get?"

"Very close. Is that bad?

"Depends on your point of view. Didn't the lady give you a hint?"

"Yes. I'm sure it slipped out. A crack about if we got much lower, sperm banks would be the most profitable pharmaceutical business in the twenty-first century. I wasn't worried. 67 million sperm seemed like a lot to me. Isn't it?"

"Not in nature's ball park. The average sperm count was 113 million per milliliter when the study was started in 1940."

"Over a forty percent drop in fifty years. Wow. That's amazing."

"If that's true, everybody ought to know about it. Everything we're studying ought to relate to that."

We took a break. While I heated water for tea, Ben read the *Science News* article that had so disturbed me, an essay entitled "That Feminine Touch," the second installment in a two-part series by Janet Raloff.[4] I told him that the Grandmothers had shown me a similar report from the University of Florida which stated that students' sperm counts were dropping every year and no apparent reason could be found. Sally had wanted to use the data in her business report, for if our capacity to reproduce life were decreasing, she said, this was evidence that Earth's ability to support life was also on the decline. I warned her that the study could not isolate any natural causes, therefore the data might not hold up. Nevertheless, she considered it to be reason for alarm. And here Ben and I were, nearly ten years later, reading once again about the apparent threat of "drowning in a sea of estrogens."

In her series, Raloff alerts us to the fact that in recent years the scientific community has become aware that many of the chemicals with which we have polluted our environment are having profound effects on the biological processes of both nonhuman and human organisms. "These agents are everywhere," Raloff warns. Many, such as pesticides, contaminate our drinking water and foods. We unsuspectingly breathe others in urban air. A mother may unwittingly pass some hormone-mimicking pollutants on to her child via the blood she supplies a fetus before birth and the breast milk with which she later feeds her newborn.[5]

Perhaps most alarming, as well as fascinating, is the observation that these chemicals have an "emasculating" effect on the gender characteristics of human males, and the problem begins as early as the first several weeks of gestation in the womb. Exposure to these "estrogenic" chemicals seems to impede the kind of development that is dependent on the presence of human hormones at precisely the right time during the process. The scenario goes like this.

In the earliest stages of fetal development, genetic programming determines whether or not a child is male or female; at this point, external features or internal qualities typically associated with gender have not emerged. About six weeks into the process, however, an important change takes place: the genes of the fetus may produce certain chemical communications which subsequently result in the secretion of male hormones. When the fetus is "bathed" in these, it begins to develop male genitalia and will eventually possess the characteristics commonly associated with maleness. However, if the fetus is not "bathed" — if something happens such that no hormones are triggered — the result is a child who develops female genitalia and traits (there is, of course, variation along the continuum of possibilities, depending on how much or how little of the male hormone the embryo is bathed in).[6] "Feminine development," says physiologist Richard Sharp, "is what we call the default pathway."[7] The presence of "estrogenic hormones" in our environment, and, by implication, in the womb where this process takes place, Raloff and others argue, could be what is subverting (emasculating) male development on a grand scale.

Alarmist? It is difficult to say really. But the conclusion of Raloff's article poses the question that should peak our curiosity, if not our concern. It is raised by Ana Soto, an endocrinologist at Tufts University School of Medicine, and it is the bottom line that everything comes down to:

> What is the economic cost of having a generation that cannot reproduce?

From Mother Earth's point of view, the price might be cheap. Feminine development the default pathway. Indeed. Ben wrote his response to the *Science News* articles on the newsprint:

This is for real!
We live in a sea of estrogens. Androgens too. One whiff
at the wrong time, from a miscellaneous chemical sprayed
onto land to make crops or pigs or cows or chickens grow
faster, or to kill weeds, or to do other good deeds. A whiff in a
factory, shop, lavatory, school. Chemicals that are supposed to
save us time, make us richer!
    Good God. One whiff at the wrong time. Does what?
Emasculates an alligator, a bird, a fish. Maybe a little. Maybe
a lot. It slowly eats its way up the food chain to humans,
creeping in through skin, all the orifices, all the membranes.
The news is that the human capacity to reproduce itself is
going down. Maybe it's coincidence. "No hard data yet," one
scientist says.

EXCITEMENT OF REAL LEARNING

I decided to try another of Helen's teaching techniques: playing devil's advocate. Helen loved to argue
against "the facts," and in the process she was able to get
her students to do the teaching.

"Teach me," she would say.

The students would lean forward in their desks,
straining to get across their ideas. They experienced the
taste of making connections and the excitement of real
learning.

    "Teach me," I said to Ben. "I don't believe any of
it. There must be a better explanation."
    "Lots of better ones," Ben said. "Nobody believes
estrogenic pollution is causing the sperm count of males to
drop! For alligators, maybe. Not humans. That's exciting."
    "Exciting? I don't get it. What's exciting about emas-
culating a species?"

"We agree that we don't believe this," Ben said. "Or let's pretend we don't. Then, we can get on to something important. Something that is exciting, if you look at it just the right way."

I thought my "teach me" technique was backfiring (even though it was taking place in my imagination). I experienced the same reaction that day when Ben visited the Council of Grandmothers, when he pointed to the graph and said, "Who would want to live there, if they could live here." The place he wanted to live was "now" -- the "now" when bankruptcy seems imminent.

He was ahead of me once more. I was still caught in the "game," the good guys against the bad, "let's solve this problem once and for all." From Ben's perspective, Earth's management system was simply doing its thing. No moral judgments. No villains. No scapegoats. There were no guarantees. A thing worked or it didn't. Self-reflective consciousness is a borderline case. It is nice to have for a planet interested in thinking, but not essential for life.

A large whiff of the right, or wrong, "environmental hormone" at the right, or wrong, time (depending on your perspective), could snuff out Earth's current self-reflective, thinking species. The planet could snooze for another millennium and enjoy a time of healing. This human birth control could very well be brought about by a self-administered overdose of "better chemistry for better living."

"Poetic justice," Ben said. "Like the hole in the ozone."
"I don't get the connection," I said.
"Remember Ian McHarg? The grandmother who played his role was tough. Said one cell had become a cancer.

Us humans. What causes the hole in the ozone? Humans. What comes through the hole? Radiation. Radiation therapy that can cure the causes of Earth's cancer.

"I think McHarg was talking Einstein's language — thinking in a new manner, getting away from the mechanistic model, the clockwork universe. We can never fix the Earth. But Earth can heal herself. Radiation therapy, birth control, whatever it takes."

"Teach me," I said.

"You're the teacher. The environmentalist," Ben said.

"I'm in kindergarten. I didn't even know Earth's business was life."

"That's because of the hole in your cheese."

"Cheese or ozone?" Ben was losing me again.

"Cheese. A Swiss cheese reality. We each look into our private hole in space. It's an infinite cheese. You never see exactly what you think you see. You never look from exactly where you think you're looking."

Ben hunched forward in his chair. Teaching me. Excited.

"Even scientists don't observe enough of the cheese to make their observations meaningful. Useful, maybe. But nothing to bet your life on."

He closed his eyes. I knew enough to keep quiet. I had seen Helen do that, too, wait for thoughts in others to jell. But this other? Who was he? A figment of my imagination? My own mind moving down out of the attic of my being?

"What the Grandmothers taught me," Ben said, "is that space goes both ways. That makes the cheese really interesting. The hole we look out of is also a hole inside us. We live where two realities intersect, touch. Each reality is like a cone. It expands inside us and away from us. It gets infinitely bigger until we and everything are one.

"Each hole is different, but each contains everything

we need. Good and evil. Male and female. We can never be so screwed up that we can't — if we get a whiff of just the right stuff — that we can't wake up."

Ben was angling back toward the implications of bathing our Swiss cheese reality in a sea of estrogens.
    "Do you know the part I liked best about the Science News *articles?"*
    "I have no idea," I said.
    "The letters from readers. Swiss cheese letters."[8]
    He explained.
    "One writer, a chemical engineer, scolded the editor. He charged that the articles were misleading and biased because they were not peer-reviewed. The sea of estrogens was 'Greenpeace style pseudo-science,' he said.
    "One complained that another hormone-mimicking chemical was not mentioned. Somatotropin, a hormone to boost milk production in cows, has been approved for use by dairies in the U.S.
    "Another respondent objected to the use of the term 'default pathway' to describe the 'feminine way.'
    "One woman felt that the title 'That Feminine Touch' was misleading, because it is 'man-made' estrogens that are polluting the environment. The problem is not a feminine one. A similar objection was made to the idea of 'Mother Nature exerting a feminizing influence.' Mother Nature is merely responding to by-products of human technology. Technology is at fault.
    "Two writers looked out of the cheese with a broader perspective. One suggested that 'eliminating some of the (human) players from the reproductive game can only be a boon to nature, while the other, a woman from Vermont, hit closest to home. She used humor. She asked if man-made environmental pollution could be sterilizing males? 'Non-

sense!' She answered her own question. 'I ask you: Would Daddy Warbucks and his good American buddies do a thing like that to themselves. Of course not. It's just anticapitalist propaganda from tree-hugging environmentalists in cahoots with the godless feminists, that's all.'"

And there you have it, according to Ben, a microcosm of the cross-currents of consciousness at work in the Swiss cheese reality. Each view is perfectly valid from its particular hole in the cheese.

Ben's point is that no matter how astute, how sincere, how caring we are, our view is limited. We see only a tiny bit of the whole cheese. But the whole is there, all around us, inside us.

Earth's cancer is not the result of evil intentions. It is caused by good people doing what they believe to be good things, each from their own hole in the cheese. But as we approach the dawn of a new century, perhaps the most important thing for us to realize is this: Earth's cancer is caused primarily by people who, despite the presumed validity of their own perspectives, no longer know who they are, men and women who have lost their story.

In the chapters that follow, we will explore ways in which we might recapture a mythology, a story, that rises up from "the basement" of our existence and gives our life meaning.

NOTES

1. John Nolt, *Down to Earth* (Washburn, TN: Earth Knows Publications, 1995) 145.

2. The Earth Literacy Communion has no formal structure; many of its members already belong to a number of "organizations," perhaps too many. The char-
acter of a "communion" is more akin to an extended
family, where coming together is a celebration. We
gather to share, commiserate, and create — we try to
help each other. This book and the Earth Knows
seed-book publishing venture are both family products of the Earth Literacy Communion.

3. Jean Houston told this story at a workshop attended
by Helen Wallace on Miami Beach. Helen and the
other participants were asked to imagine themselves
as prehistoric reptiles living in the sea. One by one
they slithered out onto the beach. They struggled to
crawl on all fours, then balance themselves precari-
ously on two feet. Helen reported: "It was a mind
blowing experience. I literally exploded out of my
basement!" Jean Houston repeats the story in an
interview with Michael Toms, entitled "The Possible
Human" (available from New Dimensions Foundation, P.O. Box 569, Ukiah, CA 95482-0569).

4. In "The Gender Benders" (*Science News*, vol. 145
[January 8, 1994]: 24-27), Raloff discusses the effects
that "environmental hormones" seem to have had
on the biological processes, primarily reproduction
and sexual development, in species as diverse as
alligators, gulls, and rainbow trout. The second article in the series, "That Feminine Touch (*Science
News*, vol. 145 [January 22, 1994]: 56-58) suggests
that human exposure to many toxic contaminants
may result in similar "feminizing" trends in males,
for example, a lowered sperm count and a higher

incidence of testicular cancer in industrial countries where pesticides and other pollutants are commonly used. These chemicals, she suggests, possess the functional attributes of female hormones.

5. Raloff, "That Feminine Touch," 56.

6. For a very readable explanation of this process, see Anne Moir, *Brain Sex: The Real Difference Between Men and Women* (New York: Delta Publishing, 1989), chapter 2. Moir makes it clear (in a way that Raloff does not in her admittedly brief article) that the hormonal bath occurring around the sixth week of development is the key factor in whether or not an XY (genetically male) *or* an XX (genetically female) fetus will develop into a characteristically male child. An XY *or* an XX fetus that is not bathed will develop as a female.

7. Raloff, "That Feminine Touch" 56.

8. As one might imagine, the combination of environmental and gender dynamics in Raloff's two articles created no small controversy among the journal's readership. Letters to the Editor ranged from supportive to vitriolic. See *Science News*, vol. 145 (April 2, 1994): 211, 220.

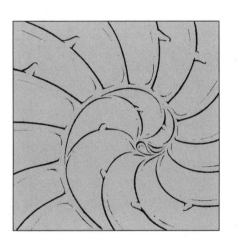

The cosmos could not possibly be explained as a dust of unconscious elements, on which life, for some incomprehensible reason, burst into flower — as an accident or as a mould. But it is fundamentally and primarily living, and its complete history is ultimately nothing but an immense psychic exercise.... From this point of view man is nothing but the point of emergence in nature, at which this deep cosmic evolution culminates and declares itself.... He is the flame of a general fermentation of the universe which breaks out suddenly on the earth.

Pierre Teilhard de Chardin
"The Spirit of the Earth"[1]

3

COMPLETING THE GRANDMOTHERS' REPORT

Like the Grandmothers, the diminutive Dominican nun came with string.

When I first saw her, she was a tousle of straw-colored hair and twinkling eyes. The rest of her disappeared behind a towering oak lectern on the stage of a barn-like meeting room. She was keynote speaker at a Conference on Christianity and Ecology held at a remote retreat center in northern Indiana.

Before I heard Sister Miriam Therese MacGillis speak, I wondered why I was there. The conference was one activity I had listed on my application for a sabbatical leave. My leave proposal was vague. I mentioned Einstein's warning: master a new manner of thinking or drift into catastrophe. I didn't mention the depression I was feeling, so strongly that it was often difficult for me to go to my office at the Environmental Center, a place I loved and had helped to build with volunteers.

Ben, after Helen moved to a nursing home in Michigan, I resigned as director of the Environmental Center. Once, I tried to find you. None of the nearby middle schools had recorded a field trip to the Center the day of the Grandmothers' meeting. I gave up the idea that I would ever see you again. Perhaps some day you will read this book. If you do, I hope you will be satisfied with my answers to your questions.

Helen's last gift to me was the taped interview with Jean Houston that I mentioned earlier. Her words continued to have a profound effect on me:

> What we are, compared to what we think we are, is so much vaster. It's as though we are living in the attic of ourselves with the first, second, third and fourth floors relatively uninhabited and the basement locked except when it explodes.

My basement seemed to be exploding. I still believed that the things the Environmental Center was doing were important — teaching the "facts" about nature, introducing students to appropriate technologies, how to prepare food organically, how to compost. My problem was not with the Center, it was with my own thinking.

My attic thinking was a "how to" mentality. I still thought we humans could fix whatever we broke. The explosion in my basement had to do with healing, not fixing. It had to do with reassessing the fundamental assumption that guided my life: that humans are in charge, and it is our job to manage the planet.

The last time I saw Helen, she and Sally performed a ritual in Helen's backyard whereby I was designated an honorary member of the Council of Grandmothers. As far as I know, the Council never met again. Along with Jean Houston's tape, Helen gave me a card on which she printed the words of a rabbi:

> God so loved a story, he created humans.

"Remember, Mac," she told me, "facts don't have meaning, except in a story."

I held up the card she had given me. "Are you, Helen Wallace, telling me that God is a he?" I tried to spark her old fire. The gender question was a touchy one for the Grandmothers.

"God's a *he* in the rabbi's story." Helen managed a smile and winced. "But it's a great story. You see, facts don't matter. Do they?"

SEARCH FOR A STORY

My sabbatical leave was a search for a story, a story in which the facts, the "how-to's" I had devoted my life to, would fall easily into place and give meaning to whatever I did next.

Before working with the Council of Grandmothers, I could not have imagined silence as a discipline for learning. Now I was being instructed everywhere to sit quietly and observe my thoughts. I was learning that to understand the inner subjective world was as important as comprehending the outer objective world. I went to Dayspring Retreat Center near Washington D.C., then to Wellspring. I spent time in silent retreat, in a discerning community, exploring what my calling might be this side of midlife crisis. I also participated in an Enneagram workshop and enrolled in the United Methodist Academy for Spiritual Formation. By the time I arrived in the backwoods of Indiana, I was ready. I had collected new parts for the puzzle and was prepared to receive Sister Miriam's gift of a new story.

Miriam was careful to point out that she was passing on a gift she had received from Father Thomas

Berry. Berry, the cultural historian and "geologian," received the gift from Pierre Teilhard de Chardin. Chardin, in turn, discovered the gift in his studies as a scientist. Early in this century, Chardin brought together, synthesized in his own psyche, two stories: the *empirical creation story* revealed by the prophets of the natural sciences, and the *intuitive creation story* revealed by the prophets of religion.

In Teilhard's day, roughly a half century after the publication of Darwin's *Origin of Species*, the empirical story offered a new, and somewhat threatening, understanding of our beginnings. As the Scopes Monkey Trial (1925) so clearly demonstrated, it appeared that there were in fact two creation accounts, one provided by the sciences, the other by religion. Teilhard was the first to try to synthesize the two, conceiving the cosmos as the ongoing development and dispersion of consciousness, a process that would eventually reach its culmination in what he called "the Omega point." Humans, as "the point of emergence in nature where this deep cosmic evolution declares itself,"[2] have the opportunity and the responsibility to be co-creators in this process, to usher in through their spiritual vocation the next stage of this unfolding universe. This was the tradition to which Thomas Berry and Miriam Therese MacGillis belonged, and one with which I was soon to become acquainted.

ANOTHER TEACHER

I was in the barn-like auditorium in Indiana to listen to Miriam MacGillis tell a new story. Ben, I was there because of questions you had asked me that I couldn't answer. In the introduction to her keynote address, Miriam explained why she was there: she embarked on her own personal journey after a young girl asked her questions that she was unable to answer. Miriam, whose Dominican mother house is in New Jersey, had been an art teacher, and the young girl was one of her students. Miriam loved to draw, to paint, and to teach, and she was quite certain about the nuances of her faith. In short, she was content with her world. It seemed almost too good to be true.

She discovered it wasn't true. Her doubts began soon after her young charge began asking questions about the Vietnam War. Was it justifiable? Whose side was God on? What about the student protests? World hunger? Then the girl asked about the environment. Miriam was dumbfounded, unable to answer such compelling queries.

Miriam had assumed that those in charge of her community, her nation, her world, knew what they were doing. They did not. And now this student's questions were alerting her to the fact that for the last several years of her life she had been living in a trance. Even her religious faith was shaken. I identified with her feelings.

"This child," Miriam said, "knew more about the real world than I did. She had a deeply formed conscience about the immorality of war, and the Vietnam war in particular. My world fell apart. I left teaching, and became involved with work for peace and justice. In 1977, at a conference I had helped to plan, I heard Thomas Berry deliver a paper on Contemplation and World Order. I couldn't have repeated a single thing Thomas said, but I knew that everything he had said was true. And I knew my life was changed.

"A little later our Dominican community inherited Genesis Farm in Blairstown, New Jersey. I moved onto the land. I began to explore one of the most sacred vocations on Earth: agriculture. Later I asked Thomas Berry if he would guide me in a directed reading course on Bioregionalism — a new way to understand agriculture within the context of the Earth's ability to grow food."

When Miriam finished speaking, I did something I had never done before. I pushed my way (or did I float?) down the aisle and shook her hand. I told her that the story she had told had given me hope. Then I asked her to teach me.

THE EMPIRICAL CREATION STORY

Miriam told us a creation story that explained in scientific terms her own personal creation story. It did not leave out the non-material half of reality. It was the story of the journey of the universe. That journey had both a physical and a spiritual dimension from its very beginning. The empirical story of science was giving shape to a new cosmology, a revelation that encompassed and honored all of the creation stories of Earth's people. Miriam saw her Genesis story of creation embellished, not diminished, by the new discoveries and revelations of modern physics. At both the physical and spiritual level, the journey was personal. It could be experienced. That was its great power.

Ben, as I listened to Miriam, I imagined you, Helen, Sally and all the Grandmothers in the auditorium with me. Miriam was completing their story -- the 100-Million-Year Business Report. She drew the Grandmothers' string back beyond the birth of Earth, beyond the birth of the first mother suns, back beyond the birth of helium and hydrogen atoms to the beginning, the beginning of all beginnings.

Even the Grandmothers' planetary management system was included. Billions of years before there was life on this planet, feedback loops were functioning. In the new story, an unbroken thread was woven through every step in the creation process. I saw (felt, really) how that thread connected me to every breakthrough, not just blue-ribbon breakthroughs on a 100-million-year string graph, but on a string stretching 15 billion years into the past. Where the Grandmothers focused merely on the story of our planet, Miriam enlarged the picture to include the history of the universe, from Big Bang to the present. Her narrative connected me, beyond space and time, to every being that exists, and to every being that has ever existed.

"We are in trouble," Miriam said. "Earth is in trouble because our old story, which gave life meaning, no longer works. Our assumptions about reality are inaccurate. That is why good people, with the best of intentions, are making decisions that are so disastrous.

"The gift Thomas Berry gave me was a creation narrative that included both the discoveries of the empirical sciences and the wisdom of the world's spiritual traditions, that did not leave out the great tribal era, the indigenous shaman and the Grandmothers' Council. These ancient ones knew in an intuitive way what physicists are learning today."

The puzzle was coming together for me. All the facts in my picture of reality were starting to make sense. The universe is and has been proceeding from simple to complex, from atoms to molecules to matter to mother suns to galaxies to suns with planets to planets with one-celled life to conscious life. The story is eternal, unending. The universe is in process.

As I listened to Miriam, I began to imagine the process she was describing as two rivers, both flowing out of the same primordial event. According to the natural sciences, the Big Bang was the womb out of which the universe was born. One river flowing out of this event was material reality, the other the river of spirit.

For most of the history of the universe, these two rivers seemed to meander on their own separate courses. One flowed underground, invisible, seeping through the pores of atoms imperceptibly. The other expanded outward over every landscape, creating new atoms, new substances, new vistas. As the universe became more complex, the two rivers began to flow as one, and eventually out of this unity of matter and spirit, a planet awakened. Life began. In the Milky Way galaxy, planet Earth, alone in starlit cosmic solitude, began its task of self-discovery.

Eventually, as consciousness grew into self-consciousness, all of Earth's people came to take part in this task. They invented stories to explain a world in which they felt both "at-one-with" and "separate-from." These were myths to tell them who they were, where they came from, and why they were here. No matter how primitive and illogical the stories may seem to us today, each provided an important piece in the puzzle that each culture endeavored to assemble. Each was a way of interpreting where the universe was going. But each was a "Swiss cheese reality," limited in its perception, bound to the relativity of social and historical context. These belief systems were, and still are, the means by which humans organize themselves, their thoughts, their observations, their explanations.

I like to think of these various myths, these ways of explaining reality, as "tricklets," springs flowing up out of the Earth. They are the stories of religion, of spirit. They are also the stories of science, of matter. They become vein-like tributaries that flow into the great story of creation itself, into the two rivers of physical and nonphysical reality. To understand the energy of an atom, the origin of life, the meaning of death, the delusion of consciousness, the function of a human being, we need both kinds of stories.

Ben, you helped bring the two rivers of reality together for me. I wish you could have heard Miriam's talk. Do you see how the Grandmother's string and Miriam's string are the same?

•   •   •

I stared at the empty chair. Suddenly Ben was there, grinning.

"I have a surprise for you," he said.

"What's your surprise?" I asked.

"I've already read Thomas Berry's book The Dream of the Earth. *A math teacher, of all people, gave extra credit for doing a paper on the New Cosmology. We were studying Chaos theory and modeling fractals. My teacher said Berry's essays were better than our math books. I thought so too."*

"Interesting," I said. "What did you do with what you learned?"

"Do? I got an 'A' in math," he said.

"I mean, if Berry's story applied in math, it ought to apply in other subjects. Didn't you..."

53

"I didn't find out," Ben said. "None of my other profs seemed interested. One warned me against reading New Age drivel."

"The best professors I know are interested," I said. "Their problem is how to fit big concepts like Berry's into the content of their courses."

Ben shook his head.

"But shouldn't big concepts fit everywhere?" he said. "Berry says Earth is our teacher. What else should education be about?"

"Yes, big concepts should fit everywhere," I said. "But we chop education into bits and pieces. Every discipline gives you its piece to the puzzle. When you have all the pieces, they don't fit together. The big picture gets lost through the cracks."

"So, what's the solution? You're the educator."

"I need your help. That's why I'm asking you," I said.

"You're serious, aren't you?"

"Yes," I said, "but in a playful way. I don't know enough to be deadly serious. I want an assignment from you. How can I make this practical?"

Ben leaned toward me, eyes bright.

"Okay. I need a more visual perspective. How about charts? Could you show the universe story on a map of some kind? Make it personal, like the Grandmothers did with their graph?"

"Miriam," I told Ben, "has already created a personal map of the empirical creation story. She calls it a cosmic walk. Her 'walk' completed my sabbatical leave and started me on a new path.

"I would like to share my experience of the cosmic walk with you."

I let Ben fade out of my vision. Again, I felt gratitude to Helen. She had given me an invaluable tool.

NOTES

1. Pierre Teilhard de Chardin, "The Spirit of the Earth," in *Human Energy* (New York: Harcourt Brace Jovanovich, 1969) 23.

2. Teilhard's vision of the empirical universe is perhaps best represented in his book *The Phenomenon of Man* (New York: Harper & Row, 1959), or the more theological work *The Divine Milieu* (New York: Harper & Row, 1960).

3. For information about workshops and a newsletter on Earthkeeping, contact the North American Conference on Christianity and Ecology, P.O. Box 40011, St. Paul, MN 55104. For information on conferences and grants to develop courses in science and religion, contact the John Templeton Foundation Science and Religion Course Program, Southern Region, Purdue University, Calumet, IN 46323-2094.

The beginning of the universe
Is the mother of all things.
Knowing the mother, one also knows the sons.
Knowing the sons, yet remaining in touch
    with the mother,
Brings freedom from the fear of death.

•   •   •

Do you think you can take over the universe
and improve it?
I do not believe it can be done.

The universe is sacred.
You cannot improve it.
If you try to change it, you will ruin it.
If you try to hold it, you will lose it.

Lao Tzu
Tao te Ching, 52, 29[1]

4

WALKING THE COSMIC STRING

As an artist, Miriam could tell the universe story and picture it, too. Like Helen, she illustrated the story experientially, with string, candles, symbols and sounds.

I was one of the workshop participants who responded to Miriam's invitation to a cosmic walk. I returned to the barn-like auditorium early and watched her unwind the history of the universe out of a pale white ball of string. She lit a candle at one end to symbolize the Big Bang — this is where the walk would begin. The string coiled outward in a spiral like the arched rib of a Chambered Nautilus.

Miriam lit more candles for each breakthrough along the way. These spikes of light served as reminders of great events in the universe story. Most of the candles were concentrated near the far end of the string. The smell of smoke triggered memories in me. I saw Helen light a candle as the Grandmothers formed a circle under a pine tree. I imagined I heard a mockingbird.

A tape recorder played voices from the forest and the sea. As we waited for our turn to begin, we heard a whippoorwill, then a wolf, an owl and a humpback whale. Recorded sounds of nature were accompanied by lonely flutes and the distant throb of drums. Miriam gave instructions, telling us which event in history each candle represented. Printed cards under each flame defined each watershed. We were invited to go to the beginning and walk the story.

Leaving the first candle, I felt as though I were walking a tightrope. For ninety percent of the journey the candles were spaced far apart. The first hydrogen atoms jelled out of an unimaginably hot radioactive soup behind me.

Miriam reminded us that billions of billions of billions of discreet atoms were working together within us in order for us to participate in this journey, that as we walked, atoms were flying away from us. We were constantly exchanging atoms with the world around us; in a few years, every atom currently in my body would be replaced.

As I walked, I formed thoughts out of the flow of atoms that was me. I thought about you, Ben. As I sauntered along the string, your words echoed in my consciousness:

All this was preparation. Who would want to live in the time of preparation if they could live now?

CELEBRATING THE CURVE

As I walked the string, I followed the mysterious curvature of space. Here, in some distant past, the future of the universe had hung in the balance. If the universe had emerged any faster, matter could not have formed. If it had emerged any slower, all matter would have collapsed back on itself. Thomas Berry, Miriam's cosmic choreographer, said we should celebrate that emergent moment, celebrate the attraction the curve holds for all subjects of the universe. We should rejoice in the affection it engenders in human hearts.

I reached the candle of mother suns. These exploding supernovas seeded the expanding universe with chemical molecules that would be needed for life. I looked back. The pale white line was like an umbilical cord.

The string united us. Other workshop participants walked ahead of me and behind me, but I was linked to them by this common bond. We were united in a swirl of atoms leading backward through time and space, an arrow of light stretching back to the first hydrogen atoms.

I remembered something Einstein said when he was old. He said he would like to spend the rest of his life contemplating the nature of light. I thought I understood why as I walked the cosmic walk. The candles commemorating different events reminded me that these breakthroughs were recorded in me, stored in the chemistry of the atoms I exchanged with the world around me, in the genes which linked me to all my ancestors.

When I thought about the string in terms of its physical dimension, I knew it was at least 15 billion light years long. When I thought about it in terms of its nonphysical dimensions, I knew it was an instantaneous creation. It was being re-created every moment. Within the string there was a tunnel of reality that did not conform to measurements of time and space. I existed also in this spaceless tunnel of light. I wondered if that unbounded realm was the nature of light that Einstein so wanted to contemplate, the realm of spirit and soul.

To the degree I could become aware of this realm of reality, I could feel a oneness with each candle. I could sense that the entire story was being re-enacted in me at each instant. This was different from recording events in history books, or preserving fossils in layers of rock. This sense of oneness with the whole, with the One, was the intuitive source of all spiritual traditions.

THE SCIENTIFIC AGE

As I approached the candle marking the scientific age, I remembered Miriam's speech earlier in the day. Empirical science was in the latter half of the twentieth century confirming the oneness of creation. This was not its original intent. Natural scientists as far back as Aristotle had always presumed that phenomena can and should be understood in purely physical terms. By breaking down the machine into its component parts, modern scientists sought to control and manipulate Earth. In all of industrialized civilization we still do.

According to this mechanistic view, environmental problems are breakdowns in the machine. The hole in the ozone, for example, is merely a defect that needs to be repaired. In the past few years, *Science News* has reported various technological fixes for this problem. One involved flying several hundred jet planes each year into the stratosphere to release 50,000 tons of ethane. According to theoretical models, an annual dose of ethane could halt much ozone depletion caused by CFC pollution. But introducing yet another chemical into the atmosphere, scientists agreed, might cause other undetermined problems. The plan, for the present, is shelved, but in all of this we find the rallying cry of the scientific age: technological solutions for technological problems.

Ben, my cosmic walk prepared the way for my imaginary dialogue with you. You were right to call the ozone hole a wound rather than a mechanical defect. Chemical pollutants we throw "away" come back to haunt us. Chemicals dumped in the stratosphere come back as "radiation therapy." Chemicals dumped in the Earth come back as "chemotherapy," concentrating in our food chain and drinking water. There is no "away." There is no "other" in our finely balanced planetary organism. There is only "us."

As I approached the candle commemorating the splitting of the atom, I wondered how long Earth's cure would take. Could my grandchildren's generation transform the cancer, mutate it into a better fitting species? Where did the impulse that brought the grandmothers together come from? What accident of fate brought you, Ben, to their last session? Why did a young girl choose Miriam to ask her disturbing questions?

The Grandmothers would say that the answer to these questions depends on your model of reality. In their model three functions guided Earth's business of life. These three, interacting as one, sustained life on Earth. They provided the give and take, the feedback loops, and the enriching energies that made Earth a cosmic oasis for four billion years. Interestingly, what they arrived at was not too far removed from the conclusions of Miriam's esteemed mentor.

THOMAS BERRY'S THREE PRINCIPLES

In Thomas Berry's empirical model of creation, three principles guided the unfolding universe from the beginning.

The first is *differentiation*. According to this principle, the universe is coded to become more and more diverse in its component parts. There is within the creative process a drive away from uniformity and toward maximum complexity and creativity.

The second principle is *interiority*. In Berry's estimation, the universe has had from its inception a non-material, spiritual dimension. At its deepest interior, everything has its own truth, and discloses, reveals, its own profound inner mystery. Nothing is confined by the bonds of space and time. In this realm of reality, we can experience our oneness with the whole, and with each of the parts of all creation.

The third principle is *communion* or *community*, which states simply that the universe has been from the very beginning in communion with itself. No differentiated interiority could exist alone. It could only exist as a member of a bonded community which has evolved mutually with itself. As the complexity of communion increased, consciousness was able to break through.

EARTH'S AWAKENING, OUR AWAKENING

I looked back at the cluster of candles crowded behind me. These commemorated the first single-celled organisms on Earth, then multicellular beings that reproduced by division, then the first real parents that reproduced by sexual union. Parenthood made possible new combinations of DNA. By combining and recombining the genes of life, limitless new possibilities opened up, possibilities for differentiation, interiority, and community/communion.

What was the purpose of so many new possibilities? At its deepest interiority, where was the universe going? Where was Earth going?

The British scientist James Lovelock believes that at its most fundamental level Earth is not a planet of dead matter inhabited by living systems. Rather, Earth is a living system itself. Herself. Lovelock even provides her with a name: *Gaia*, the ancient Greek goddess of the Earth. Gaia regulates, on a grand scale, her own life functions, her own body temperatures, the salinity in her oceans. Her oceans create one interconnected planetary circulatory system that flows through every living creature. My body, yours, everyone's body, consists mainly of salt water. Gaia regulates the flow of oxygen and carbon dioxide in and out of her lungs - and in and out of our lungs. She regulates the chemistry of her bodily functions and her immune system. Lovelock concludes that the scientific evidence suggests:

> Earth's atmosphere is not merely a biological product, as oxygen often is, but more probably a biological construction - like a cat's fur, or a bird's feathers; an extension of a living system, designed to maintain a chosen environment.[2]

If Lovelock is correct, then our prior assumptions about this "machine" upon which we have existed for millennia need radically to be revised.

As I approached the end of the string, I thought about what Lovelock meant by a biological construct. I thought about the curvature of space, about its allurement, about how a group of elderly women came together in the last years of their lives to seek a model of reality that they could believe in. I thought about a priest who spent his lifetime doing the same thing.

The auditorium doors were open and a sudden breeze caused the candles to flicker. I glanced back along the path that I had traversed. So much preparation was needed for this moment of new possibilities. One species on Earth was granted a certain amount of freedom from Earth's hardwired management system. Humans were given the opportunity of choice, and it seems by all accounts to have been a mistake. But a new chapter in the story was about to begin. The last candle celebrated humankind's awakening.

What does it mean to awaken? To think in a new manner? To imagine? To judge? At that moment, I felt the presence of my grandchildren. I heard Aubrey Elizabeth's excited voice. "Poppa, I called you with my own mouse!"

The awakening will require much intellectual work, sensitivity, and sophistication, but when achieved, it will seem simple. It will be available to all who are not totally closed to a new manner of thinking. The simplest of us will be able to take a deep breath and say, "Ah, yes. Of course. That's how it is. How could it be otherwise?"

I passed the last candle and went outside. Overhead in the oak trees, cicadas were singing. Their chorus seemed a fitting finale for my cosmic walk. Or was it? Were the night-singing insects heralding an end or a new beginning? Both, I believe.

NOTES

1. Lao Tzu, *Tao te Ching*, trans. by Gia-Fu Feng and Jane English (New York: Vintage Books, 1989) 54, 31.

2. James Lovelock, interviewed by Michael Toms for New Dimensions Radio and available on audio cassette from New Dimensions Foundation, P.O. Box 569, Ukiah, CA 95482-0569. Lovelock's books include *Ages of Gaia* (New York: W.W. Norton & Co., 1994), and *Gaia: A New Look at Life on Earth* (Oxford: Oxford University Press, 1987).

We do not know how ambitious to be, what or how much we may safely desire, when or where to stop. I knew a barber once who refused to give a discount to a bald client, explaining that his artistry consisted, not in the cutting off, but in the knowing when to stop. He spoke, I think, as a true artist and a true human. The lack of such knowledge is extremely dangerous.... But ignorance of when to stop is a postmodern epidemic: it is the basis of "industrial progress" and "economic growth." The most obvious practical result of this ignorance is a critical disproportion of scale between the scale of human enterprises and their sources in nature.

Wendell Berry
"Getting Along With Nature"[1]

5

LEARNING TO BREATHE UNDER WATER

In the star brightness of that Indiana country night, I saw the string of my life clearly. I understood what I would have to do. I started then to make plans to return to work.

Ben, I also knew why I felt guilty when you asked why nobody had told you before. I wanted you to know I couldn't have told you. I was anxious to explain that I didn't know either, until now.

Of course, I couldn't have told you. You were a stranger to me. So why did I feel so defensive?

KEEPING THE TRANCE GOING

I walked away from the flickering light coming from the open barn door. Bursts of cicada music moved with me. I sat on some grass at the edge of an open field. The stars hung just an arm's length above the tree tops. Every star was there, just as they had been in my childhood on country nights during school vacations.

Miriam's cosmic walk had brought back the memories. I had felt connected way back when. How much had I forgotten while I was growing up, while I was being educated and pursuing two careers? I had lived in the same hypnotic trance that Miriam had talked about, and I saw the ways in which I contributed to keeping the trance going. One of my careers was in journalism, the other in education.

When I worked as a writer and an editor, I thought I was providing a valuable service to society. As a newspaper man, I was communicating reality. We journalists give people the information they need in order to make up their own minds, to vote intelligently, to live lives that make sense.

Sitting under stars that I could almost touch, I saw my career in journalism in a new light. I had not been communicating reality. I had been perpetuating the sound track by which society legitimized its assumptions — assumptions based on an old manner of thinking. It was the sound track of authorities, the same men in high places that Helen and the Grandmothers rebelled against.

Enough is enough.

The revelation that the reality I had believed and communicated was an illusion did not come as a complete surprise. In retrospect, I recall having had doubts.

I remember the enthusiasm I felt when I was asked to begin a journalism department in a community college. I planned to do some things differently, and I did. But I continued to transmit an accepted vision of the world, the momentary reality that flashes by in headlines and on television screens. This was the anthropomorphic reality dissected in college textbooks, buried under layers of psychological and social interpretation, and it had the blessing of most scientists. In perpetuating this vision, I believed I was giving students the big picture they needed.

In retrospect, I see how small the picture really was. I was part of the "hooking" process, playing the game that had nothing to do with where the universe was going, or what it was about. I remember some of my best students telling me that school felt like prison to them. I tried hard to make the prison seem more appealing, to make the trance, the game, seem real.

When I became director of the Environmental Center, I took my basic model with me. The bottom line of my reality was that, on Earth, humans are in charge.

Ben, what you did for me was undermine my bottom line. The Grandmothers gave me a glimpse of a grander possibility for human participation in Earth's drama, but if it weren't for you, I probably would have lost their deeper vision. I would have simply incorporated it into my game. That day when you walked to the blackboard, you seemed to be in a trance. I thought you were in another world. I now believe that you were not in a trance at all but in the real world. If anything, you came out of society's shared trance to approach the chalk board. I now see the world I once reported on and taught about in a new light.

You were right. Total bankruptcy has to be a possibility to shake us out of our stupor. We cannot, through intellectual means alone, change the human mutation from a cancer into a better fitting species. We must learn to look within ourselves, and recall what humans have known before: that we are not mastermind fixers of a mechanical reality. Rather, we are members of the Earth community and the universe community. Members, just as our arms, legs and head are members of our bodies. But we are members with a special gift: self-reflective consciousness.

You asked what I was going to do. I have given you a partial accounting. I returned from my sabbatical leave with a plan to create an Environmental Ethics Institute at my college. The bottom line of the environmental crisis was not, I proposed, what I previously thought it to be. It was not a crisis of information, technology, economics, or political will. It was a crisis of ethics, of spirit, of soul.

TRYING TO MIMIC EARTH'S MANAGEMENT SYSTEM

Ben, I am extending an invitation to you. I want you to come see for yourself what I am doing now. Since I started this book, my hope that we might meet again has risen. Earth Knows Publications will publish and "plant" the book.

Earth Knows is one of the grassroots projects evolving at the Narrow Ridge Earth Literacy Center near Washburn, Tennessee. It grows seed books in the steep Cumberland Mountain/Norris Lake region, then distributes these wherever the wind, the post office, and friends may carry them.

Hopefully, the seeds will also be scattered in dozens of other regions, especially those with their own Earth Literacy Centers. This is one of the ways we try to mimic Earth's management system. How does a new species take root and prove itself? We think that if a seed book fills a niche, serves a purpose, it will continue to grow. If it puts into the system more than it takes out, it will migrate to new and unexpected places. In this way, this book could conceivably reach you.

If you do visit Narrow Ridge, tell Bill Nickle that I sent you. Bill directs the Narrow Ridge Center. We met by accident at a United Methodist conference at Lake Junaluska, North Carolina. I was a professor newly enrolled in kindergarten at the time, and he was a Methodist pastor also enrolled in the same grade. Neither of us knew what we were going to do with the rest of our lives.

In a similar way, at other times, and by other accidents, I met other members of the Earth Literacy Communion. Like Miriam, I no longer believe in accidents. Other members include Jim Hall, an Earthkeepers physician in Washington, D.C.; Jody Bryan, a workshop leader in North Carolina; Joe Iannone, a dean at St. Thomas University in Florida; Dan Daniel and Rick Johnson, professors at Southwestern College in Kansas; Linda Brady, a workshop leader in Idaho; and Ross McCluney, a research physicist in Florida. All of us had two things in common: we all had been compulsive planetary fixers. Now we were becoming cosmic amphibians, and as such we would have to learn to "breathe under water," to inhabit two worlds.

LOVE, TOUGH LOVE

Ben, your invitation is to come check out how well I am doing. To breathe under water, to inhabit two worlds, the first requirement is to be in love — like Helen Wallace was in love. Only then can one look at the Grandmothers' Business Report for Earth and not be paralyzed by fear, by anger, by despair, by indifference.

I believe that every child is born "in love" with all that crawls and creeps and grunts, in love with dirt and leaves and rocks. All children are naturally called to become cosmic amphibians until that love is conditioned out of them, until they are taught to experience themselves as separate from the universe. They are in love until they join the adult world of delusion.

"Cosmic amphibian love" makes it possible to breathe in both the world of delusion and in the world of reality. Miriam MacGillis expresses that love best for me:

> Love is the bonding of the planet. We are beginning to understand that the human is the being in which Earth's communion is understood with awareness and freedom. That is our destiny: to be entranced by it, to love it, and become the ground of its being.
>
> And love is not love when it demands the conformity of the other. Conformity and community are diametrically opposed. Uniformity is evil; a violation of truth. If you know who you are, and you are in touch with your interiority, then you are not threatened by me if I am different. If you know who you are, then you have the capacity to delight in my differences. The more you delight in me, the more I can go into 15 billion years of energy and pull out all kinds of treasures. I will even become, at your rejoicing, capable of compassion and justice, mercy and gentleness, integrity and peace.
>
> You can bring out of me the deepest mysteries of the universe. That's love. And you can do it without even liking me. And it is this love physicists are saying we've got to learn, and to internalize in our institutions and in our education.[2]

I believe Miriam is right. We have 15 billion years of energy from which we can pull all kinds of treasures. If I am not threatened by others, I may be capable of compassion and justice, mercy and goodness, integrity and peace. But, Ben, I still feel threatened by people and institutions that do not see reality as I do. I find it difficult to delight in our differences.

AMOEBAS AND BUREAUCRATS

Lessons I learned from the author and social critic Ivan Illich are helping me. The institutions I don't like are, ironically, often like living organisms themselves. Once a bureaucracy is established to manage an institution, it takes on a life of its own.

Illich claims that, despite good intentions, bureaucracies end up creating the very problems they were established to resolve. They do so because they have all the characteristics of a colony of amoebas, except one: human institutions do not shoulder the same sense of responsibility that amoebas do! They don't have to do what amoebas have to do to stay in business. They don't have to return a profit to Earth, or be useful in the long run.

From an amoeba's point of view, human institutions in industrialized nations exist on welfare. Capitalism, Socialism, and Communism, for example, all depend on a free handout from other hard-working species in their ecosystems in order to survive. A hard-wired colony of amoebas understands the meaning of bankruptcy far better than any human. Because we are not hard-wired, we are capable of destroying the life support systems of one geographic region, and then moving on to destroy another.

Every modern society has produced obsolete institutions:

- Educational institutions created to develop independent thinking, competency and wisdom have perpetuated conformity, mediocrity and pathology.

- Religious institutions established to awaken the human psyche and celebrate the presence of the divine have promoted dehumanizing, worldly values and insensitivity to the sacredness of all creation.

- Medical institutions founded to provide compassionate service and life-giving care have instead sustained impersonal relationships and upheld death-avoidance technologies.

- Political institutions created to provide security and equal rights to all have engendered feelings of insecurity and institutionalized inequality.

- Business institutions which are to provide goods and services to meet society's real needs have wantonly promoted an artificial desire in individuals for unnecessary commodities.

Good people in institutions created for noble purposes unwittingly but methodically move civilization toward catastrophe. I am one of those people. When I see myself trapped in the same game as other human beings, I feel the "bonding love" of the universe. It tugs like a tide deep within the cells of my body, a tide that draws me back into the Earth community. As that love sucks sand from under my feet, unbalances me, I see how unbalanced we all are. We are adrift in the same boat. I see the oneness we share. In such times, differences no longer frighten me. I can rejoice in those I might even dislike. We all carry treasures, gifts given to humankind during the long journey.

THE PAST AS PROLOGUE

I see in my grandchildren treasures that will be needed. If they know the long journey they have traveled, they will be prepared. Ben, they are more like you than me. They are born amphibians.

I am seeking ways to break through the social sound track that encourages children to think that they are less than what they really are. My goal is to subvert institutions of education, religion, medicine, law, politics, and business, to prevent them from hooking my grandchildren. I believe that children who know that love is the bonding force of the planet will be alright. Even when the going is tough, they will not look for a way out: drugs, violence against others, suicide.

Ben, I want all children to understand what you helped the Grandmothers and me to understand, that what happens next depends on us, that each life is important, and all of the past up until now has been a preparation.

Miriam describes this preparation and suggests the profound question that we must answer before we move on from here.

From the first unfolding of hydrogen, helium and carbon atoms, the universe has had an exterior material dimension and an interior spiritual dimension.

You are the human in which Earth has awakened to its interior dimension, in which Earth has become spiritually aware and self-reflective. You are irreplaceable and irrepeatable.

Until now, the unfolding process depended on a finely balance automatic control. This automatic control assured the sustainability of life on Earth. With technology, humans are turning the process off of automatic and are putting it on manual. Human consciousness is taking control of the creation process itself.

The most profound question is: have humans arrived at a place where they can participate in the process of creation with the same wisdom, integrity and maturity that the universe exhibited while on automatic control?[3]

THE STRAW BALE HOUSE

Ben, when you visit Narrow Ridge, I would like for you to check out the new Seventh Generation "home place" I have created for my grandchildren. I built it with the help of friends while I was writing this manuscript. We constructed it partially out of bales of straw, and the book took longer to complete than the house!

I learned the art of straw-bale construction at a workshop sponsored by Out on Bale, (Un)Limited.[4] The instructors showed us pictures of houses and churches built over 100 years ago in Montana and Canada that are still standing today. I know what you are thinking: what about the three little pigs, the one who built his house out of straw? Yes, the wolf blew it down... but it seems the dumb pig didn't pin the bales together properly! If he'd done it right, the pig story just might have encouraged generations of kids to build with straw. Lots of trees could have been saved, forests would not have been cut, and all the animals would have been better off... including the wolf!

The building we constructed during our workshop felt just right. It was rock solid once we applied plaster over chicken wire attached to the straw. The thick, bale-sized walls had the appearance of adobe, which I love. The tightly packed bales are practically fire proof, and there is no better insulation available.

Straw is a renewable resource. At Narrow Ridge, we figure we could grow at least two houses on the upper 40 acres each summer. And with the straw, we also get a winter supply of oats and wheat. Now doesn't this sound more like the way Gaia might manage her affairs?

PRESERVING THE LAND

In addition to crops, Narrow Ridge is also growing land — land trusts. This new development is even more exciting to me than growing houses. Most of the farmers in the vicinity have long since given up making their living solely by farming. The few who do carry on the tradition do it more for sentimental reasons than of necessity. If plowing land, planting seeds, and tending cattle or sheep has been in your blood for 80 years, it's hard to stop. They do it in spite of the economic and political realities that have made the family farm a fixture of the past.

The land and the hardened grandpas and grandmas who cling to it have suffered neglect, but the memories buried deep in both farm land and farm people are rich. Even the abandoned places have lessons to teach, and perhaps these are now just beginning to flower, to take hold in the soul of this biotic community. Many fields once cultivated are now almost indistinguishable from surrounding forests, and creatures believed to have been lost forever are actually making a comeback in the region - the coyote and the Red Wolf, for example.

And people are coming back to the steep slopes around Narrow Ridge, but this time they are not coming to exploit. Not to mine, pollute, and exhaust the land. These are individuals and families rattled by what they are experiencing in cities, who shake their heads at the craziness they find themselves caught up in. They are men and women who see good people with good intentions trapped in a meaningless game that can have no good end.

So when old farms neighboring Narrow Ridge come up for sale, the owners often go first to Rev. Bill Nickle. Bill sees the land itself as his pastorate. When the first farm became available, Bill did not know what to do, but he did know what not to do. Developers were working their way north from Knoxville, coming dangerously near. Bill resolved that the land should not be bulldozed. Its memories should be preserved, as should the lessons it had to teach. The real estate market should not dictate the fate of Hogskin Valley, Log Mountain and Black Fox farm. Bill went to lawyers and learned about conservation easements which, when properly written, could head off destructive developments. With such a legally binding contract, the land itself and the creatures living there would be given rights that could be enforced in courts of law.

Ben, I think Bill was responding to the bonding force of the planet. No lesser force could have drawn him away from the work he was already doing. He had his hands full keeping the fledgling Narrow Ridge Center going. With a few volunteers and two community workers he rehabilitated two old farm houses. He constructed a resource center and a retreat house that uses only appropriate technology (that means no intrusive power lines for electricity). Sunlight is stored by photovoltaic cells in batteries and is used as electricity to pump water, provide lights, and operate small appliances. A composting toilet converts human waste into a useful by-product.

While everything is being rehabilitated, and as other construction projects continue, Narrow Ridge hosts biodynamic gardening workshops and other regional events. It also offers internships to students who want to study Earth Literacy.

A SAFETY ZONE

Ben, I am going into detail about what Narrow Ridge is doing because it is what I am doing, too. You asked what I would do, now that I know. As I approach my 70th birthday, I believe this is the best answer I can give. It is also my attempt to apply the Seventh Generation Test to my life. What will be the effect of the last decades of my life on the lives of my children seven generations into the future?

I will pass on to at least the next two generations a place. I see it as a place balanced between two worlds, a launching place for would-be cosmic amphibians. It is a safety zone where one can leave behind for a while society's sound track.

If the place seems right to any of my descendants, they will have an option to stay — at least I will have provided the launching pad. They will have to define for themselves the role they will play as citizens of Narrow Ridge's biological hamlet of the greater Earth community. That will mean joining the community as a human citizen who enriches rather than depletes.

I want my children and grandchildren to understand what it is I am trying to do. Ben, perhaps you can help me make my intentions clear. It is not my beliefs or agenda that I want to pass on as a burden to them. I believe that they have been, from the start, more amphibian than I. There are many ways and places where they could learn to "breathe under water," where they can become contributing members of Earth's community.

Ben, my motives are practical and idealistic. If the human economy is as out of sync with nature's economy as it seems, there will certainly be disruptions in the human economy. Maybe bankruptcy. These could come during my grandchildren's lives. I am one who, with good intentions, has contributed to the imbalance between the two economies. My retirement probably depends on investments that exacerbate the problem. I have friends whose retirement security already has been diminished beyond anything they imagined possible. The nest eggs for a few have been completely wiped out.

I have thought long and hard about the heritage I want to leave my grandchildren. In my present circumstances, I might leave in my will a modest reserve of stocks or bonds or cash. I have tried to imagine seven generations into the future, far beyond my society's sound track version of security. What would a colony of amoebas advise about the institutions my stocks and bonds support?

A *"HOME PLACE"*

I think I know what the amoebas would advise. When Bill Nickle sent word that the Hogskin Valley farm was for sale, I had no doubts. Bill said a trust was being set up. Narrow Ridge would hold a conservation easement that would preclude any detrimental use of the land itself. Purchasers of shares in the Hogskin Valley Land Holders Association would create their own bylaws to further define their intentions, expectations, and assumptions.

The defining process took more than three years. I am now a land holder in two land trusts affiliated with Narrow Ridge. As "land holders" we are more custodians than we are owners. A conservation easement and our own bylaws dictate our responsibilities as well as our rights. Now, with the new Black Fox property, there are three land trusts dedicated to preserving the land and learning from it.

My rights include the option to build several "home places" in the future. For the present, my straw bale structure will be used as a dormitory for Earth Literacy students who intern for a semester at Narrow Ridge. The dorm is "off the grid," which means that it is not dependent on an electric power plane or other public utilities. Composting toilets process all waste, a solar pump provides water from a well, and photovoltaic cells convert sunlight into electricity. My long-range plan is for the straw bale house and my other land holdings to provide a Seventh Generation "home place" for my grandchildren, if any of them have a need or become interested.[5]

A Seventh Generation "home place" is where someone can experience, not just speculate about, a new manner of thinking. One can meet adults who are living a new model of "success," people with credentials, qualified to make it big in the world they are leaving behind. They are choosing to swap the competitive world of the human economy for the cooperative world of nature's economy. Some live intentionally simple lifestyles on incomes of less than $8,000 a year. They seek to incorporate the principles of differentiation, interiority and communion into their daily lives.

Each person is motivated by different reasons. For some, their place will be a getaway, maybe a retirement home someday. Others want to move lock, stock and barrel as soon as they can. Some mainly want to support the work of Narrow Ridge. But I believe all see their place as more than a location on a map, property they own. It is a learning environment where they can experience the bonding force of the universe. It is part of a learning community, and Earth is the teacher.

I know that none of my immediate descendants may be drawn to this particular place. That will be alright, too. My legacy is for seven generations into the future. My larger families are the human family and the Earth family. I want to leave a place where these two can meet in communion when they are ready.

Ben, am I answering your question? I wonder if any of this applies to you wherever you are now. I would like to talk to you again. I need you to help me stay on track.

• • •

I believe Helen would have been proud of me. I was able to visualize Ben right away. He was sitting in the chair opposite me, leaning forward, elbows on his knees. "You said your motives were practical and idealistic," Ben said. "So are mine. I'm working on a Ph.D. in physics. What would I go to an Earth Literacy Center for?" "I don't know what you would go for," I said. "But I have a friend with a Ph.D. in chemistry from Harvard who went to one and stayed. You could ask him." "I'd like to do that. Who's your friend?" "Larry Edwards quit his job at the National Science Foundation. His wife Jean left a tenured teaching position in Virginia. They gave up what we call success and security to work with Miriam MacGillis at Genesis Farm in New Jersey. They are creating an Earth Literacy Center for students. They opted for another world, one that they believe is more real than the one you and I were conditioned to believe in."[6]

"I don't think the world we were taught to believe in is real," Ben said. "I doubt if any of my friends think that the way they will spend their lives is real either. We joke about it sometimes. What else can we do?"

"I can tell you what Larry and Jean did. What I'm trying to do...."

"Maybe your friends can afford the luxury of doing what they want," Ben said. "You, too. You're retired. Me, I'm in debt over my head. All my friends are. We're already hooked.

"I could recruit the best students from my classes. We'd go anywhere -- even Hogskin Valley or Jersey. Just show us jobs that make us feel good about being human. Jobs that don't diminish Earth, that don't make life more miserable for other people."

"Ben, don't get me wrong," I said. "I'm not advising you and your friends to move to Hogskin Valley or Genesis Farm. Earth needs you right where you are.

"Moving to Genesis Farm or Narrow Ridge isn't a luxury. It's more like joining a monastery back in the Dark Ages. The monks thought working with Earth's soil and working with their own souls was what was keeping the human enterprise from total collapse.

"Ben, I think that same kind of work is needed even more now than then. This time we're not just keeping human civilization from total collapse. We're keeping the human species alive."

Ben closed his eyes and I waited. I liked the fact that we didn't have to fill every minute with talk. I waited some more. Then he opened his eyes and stared into mine.

"Remember, you said we are cosmic amphibians? I like that image. I like the image of monks keeping the human experiment from going completely sour. And you're right. My place isn't at Narrow Ridge or Genesis Farm. I would like to visit. Check out the land trusts and what you're doing. See your straw bale house. I think it'd be cool to get to know your grandchildren if any of them come around.

"But I'd be a mainstream monk. Even if cities are obsolete, we can't let them fall completely apart, go into chaos. There has to be a transition not just in thinking, but in institutions."

Ben leaned back in his chair. His arms hung limp. His shoulders sagged. He waited.

"I agree," I said. "The business of human institutions and the business of Earth have to be in sync. That's Thomas Berry's point. And to do that will take mainstream monks of a special order."

"That's the order I want to be part of," Ben said. "You guys at Hogskin and Genesis can fine-tune what Earth is

84

teaching. The tough assignment will be putting Earth's lessons into action, redoing how we do business. I could get excited about that."

Ben stood up. He looked excited. He rotated his shoulders in their sockets, twisted the kinks out of his body. He looked like an athlete getting ready to go into action. I heard joints pop. I thought to myself that this was a weird thing to imagine. Then, I caught myself going through the same contortions. Ben cleared his throat.

"I want to think my generation can beat the odds Ivan Illich gives mainstream institutions. But I get my degree soon, and I'm worried. I'm interviewing for jobs. The jobs look great, at first. Then you start to ask questions, apply the Seventh Generation Test. I don't know what to do...."

Ben sat down again.

"Would you like to know what Thomas tells young people to do?" I asked.

"I would," Ben said nodding.

"Thomas Berry gives three words of advice:

SURVIVE. CRITIQUE. CREATE.

Ben grinned and asked, "So, what's that about?"

I recited what I had heard Berry say in his lectures.[7]

"To survive, you have to become competent in something. Something you feel attracted to. Mainstream monks will live their entire lives in uncertainty, in ambivalence. To live in ambivalence, you have to have a skill that you do well and like doing. If you are good at what you do, Thomas says, there is no profession, no institutional job that exists, that won't be needed. If you are competent in something, you can make a contribution. If you can make a contribution, you can survive.

"Next, critique. This means to be present to what is happening around you and how it is affecting the earth. To

continue to survive, you must be aware of what is disabling you and the rest of the natural world. You must be aware of what is enabling you to live and the rest of the natural world to live. You won't know what to do if you don't critique.

"Finally, turn your competency into creative channels. Create a viable mode of living for yourself, and for everyone else. If what you create enables others to live in a mutual relationship with all other life forms, then you have created something very *significant.*

"This is the most attractive game you play. You can have a marvelous experience. If you're looking for any kind of exciting life, Thomas says, this is it."

Ben straightened his body in his chair. He breathed deeply, hands folded in his lap.

"I like it," he said. "I think I'll be competent. I'm a survivor. I can make a contribution. But I need tools if I am going to critique. A chart showing Berry's principles of differentiation, interiority and communion would help. I need some kind of visuals to work with."

NOTES

1. Wendell Berry, "Getting Along With Nature," in *Home Economics* (San Francisco: North Point Press, 1987) 15-16.

2. Miriam Therese MacGillis, "Fate of the Earth," audio tape available from Global Perspectives, P.O. Box 925, Sonoma, CA 95476.

3. Miriam Therese MacGillis, presentation at an Earth Literacy Communion gathering at Southwestern College. The College offers Earth Literacy options and sponsors a one-semester undergraduate residency

at the Narrow Ridge Center in Washburn, Tennessee. For information, write Earth Literacy Program, Southwestern College, Winfield, KS 67156.

4. Out On Bale, (Un)Limited, publishes *The Last Straw*, a quarterly journal committed to "expanding and sharing knowledge of straw bale construction, and promoting its wider use, so that the need for durable, inexpensive, energy-efficient housing can be integrated with the need for sustainable agriculture and industrial systems to the betterment of the environment and all life forms on a planetary level." Their address is P.O. Box 4200, Tucson, AZ 85332-200.

5. For more information on Earth Literacy internships with housing in the straw bale dorm, and also retreats in the "off-the-grid" hermitages, contact the Narrow Ridge Center, R.R. 2, Box 125, Washburn, TN 37888.

6. For information on Earth Literacy programs at Genesis Farm, including an accredited graduate certificate program, write Genesis Farm Earth Literacy Center, 41A Silver Lake Rd., Blairstown, NJ 07825.

7. Berry made this presentation at a Healing the Earth (Humans, too) conference sponsored by the Institute for Pastoral Ministries at St. Thomas University. The University offers Earth Literacy options, including graduate studies with a residency at Genesis Farm. For information, contact the Institute for Pastoral Ministries, St. Thomas University, 16400 N.W. 32nd Avenue, Miami, FL 33054.

We are about the Great Work. We all have our particular work — some of us are teachers, some of us are healers, some of us in various professions, some of us are farmers. We have various occupations. But besides the particular work we do and the particular lives we lead, we have a great work that everyone is involved in and no one is exempt from. That is the work of moving on from the Cenozoic to an emerging Ecozoic Era in the story of the planet Earth....

Thomas Berry[1]

6

CHARTS TO CRITIQUE BY

Ben, like the Grandmothers and Miriam, I will start with string. I'll use it to chart one continuum that will include both universe awakenings and human awakenings. In our old manner of thinking, we separated the awakening of matter into life from the awakening of spirit into consciousness. This is the separation in our thinking that has gotten our species into trouble.

The separation was necessary, Ben. It was part of the preparation you saw in the Grandmother's graph. The first step in the evolution of human consciousness came after we began to name things. We defined objects in our world in order to think about them, just as Helen had to give you a name in order for us to talk to you.

The next step involved thinking about these objects in an organized manner, in a "useful" way. This seemed to be particularly important in what would become known as the West. We really need to state this, because not every culture felt the need to label and organize the world according to how they perceived its value. This has gotten us into trouble, but it seems as though we couldn't avoid it.

To think in an organized way, we had to classify the things we named. The ability to classify and compare was essential in order for human consciousness to make its more subtle distinctions, in order to examine things in their smallest and largest implications. The Greek philosopher Aristotle was perhaps the first systematically to undertake this task. Without these steps there could be no science, and technology would probably not have developed as we know it today. Naming, classifying, and comparing are fine as far as they go, but they don't go very far. They don't give us an understanding of what is really significant about the objects we classify. But they are essential steps to manipulating and controlling — or, at least, creating the illusion that we are in control.

The down side to classifying and controlling is that we have to narrow our field of vision. We have to leave out everything that doesn't fit the tiny model that you, Ben, called our Swiss cheese reality. That means we have to strive for uniformity. We must try to superimpose our fixed, static models on a dynamic unfolding process.

HUMAN ENTERPRISE VS EARTH ENTERPRISE

This, Ben, is where Miriam MacGillis says that evil enters the picture. In proclaiming our tiny, inadequate models as received truths of the universe, we go further and further astray. We cast the human enterprise more and more in opposition to the Earth enterprise. Miriam says:

> The Earth has evolved as a single communion, both externally in the material composition of its living fabric and internally in its psychic devel-

opment. There are no empty spaces, no islands. In that communion, the forces within all things hold everything together, but do not demand conformity. Conformity and community are diametrically opposed. Uniformity is evil.

Diversity in human consciousness is as essential to life on Earth as diversity within the mineral and animal and vegetable communities. If we do not learn this, we will continue unwittingly to live lives that violate the very process by which the universe is coded by its Creator.[2]

The classification and controlling business began in earnest with the start of the scientific age four centuries ago. It has now succeeded so well that it is in danger of going out of business. The runaway orgy of naming, classifying, and controlling was needed to complete the juvenile chapter of the human story. It narrowed our field of vision until the thing we were viewing disappeared altogether.

We were looking for a building block universe. The atom, we believed, was the smallest block. We wanted a reality we could take apart and reassemble to our specifications. We thought the universe was uniform, fixed, predictable.

The atom refused to stay still. Our agenda didn't match Earth's agenda. To cling to our agenda, we divorced our scientific selves from the deep interiority of our real selves. When physicists finally broke open the atom, it wasn't a building block. Instead, it was a window into an inner world as vast as the outer one. We discovered in the sub-atomic world, the act of measuring could change the perception of the object of our inquiry. We couldn't remove ourselves from our experiments no matter how objective we wanted to be.

At this point, some physicists began to sound like philosophers, or, worse yet, mystics. The universe was less scientific than we wanted it to be, but it was more poetic. At its interior, there was a nonmaterial dimension to reality.

Most important, it seemed that the universe was going somewhere. We were taking part in its story. We were here for a reason. We had a role to play. If a poet had said it, forget it. An artist, a musician, a prophet wouldn't have had a hearing. The new creation story was empirical. It was, as Thomas Berry said, the greatest spiritual gift of Western science. It revealed a universe that was spiritual from its beginning!

For us to understand the meaning of the story will require many different story-tellers: artists, poets, musicians, writers, composers, puppeteers, medicine men and women, shamans, mystics, theologians; as well as geologians, nuclear physicists, biochemists, geneticists, historians, anthropologists, mathematicians, linguists, systems analysts, and chart-makers.

AN EARTH LITERACY PERCEPTUAL GRID

Ben, I haven't forgotten your request. For the rest of this chapter and the next I will play chart-maker. Before beginning, though, I want to put this method of classifying and comparing in context. Each chart will be a model. It will use symbols to apply Earth Literacy concepts to the world you and I have experienced as reality.

This chapter will include five *Cone Charts*. Chapter 7 will include two *Cone Charts*. On paper the illustrations are, of course, flat. It is important to imagine each model as having dimensions of both space and time. The purpose of the cone is to provide a perceptual grid for viewing events in the universe story.

The grid that *you*, the reader, devise will be personal, incorporating your own perceptions. All of the *Cone Charts* used together will be your genealogical record. They will tell your family's 15 billion-year story. They will relate you to all the families in the universe community.

MAKING A MINIATURE OBSERVATORY

In your imagination, stretch a string back to when the universe was born -- to the birthing event that many scientists call the Big Bang. Hold on to your end of the string. At the other end, the universe of time and space is expanding outward. Visualize other strings projecting out from the point of the "Big Bang" in every direction, like the seeds in a dandelion puff. Each string is the center of an ever-expanding cone of freshly created space and time. Role a flat piece of paper into the shape of a cone and slide it over your string. The space filling the cone around your string is a model of the space/time cone of reality in which you are now located.

Your string leads from the moment of the universe's creation directly to you. The cone provides a three dimensional chart. You can record on your string the major awakenings that preceded your own. You can use your cone as a miniature observatory to observe the unfolding process that Thomas Berry describes. Each awakening is a breakthrough. Each creates the potential for more differentiated communities of matter and life. But conditions within the cone also must be ready for such a breakthrough.

No new thing is brought into being without a place being prepared for it. In your cone, you can chart the interaction of the three principles of differentiation, interiority and communion at work. This interaction prepares the expanding community for new innovations, new awakenings.

As long as the string is there, it is a symbol of the principle of interiority. It carries the memory. It passes through the center of every atom that is the center of all atoms. Around it resonates a "morphogenic field," that is, a readying force that some scientists believe carries a primordial energy too subtle to be measured. At each breakthrough in the unfolding universe, that "energy-memory" carries the blueprint of what will be needed next. It gives form and purpose to each new element of creation.

In the illustrations that follow:

Chart 1 is a cross-section of an expanding universe of strings. Each string takes with it its own space/time cone of reality.

Chart 2 is a side view of your string centered in a paper cone. The cone represents your personal space/time reality.

Chart 3 is an illustration of the process by which differentiation and communion are integral parts of every breakthrough. Each awakening is shown as a new small cone expanding around the string inside the larger cone. These could represent the first awakening of subatomic particles, or the first molecules of matter, or the first single cell living beings, or your own birth. The process of differentiation is shown by the increasing activity inside the expanding cone. More and more diverse forms evolve. These enter into more complex relationships. The communion (or community) of forms moves to higher states of creativity. At every level, from microscopic to giant suns and galaxies, there is a communion of purpose and of being.

Chart 4 is a continuum of awakenings from the primordial origin to the present. It is not to scale because the initial breakthroughs are separated by hundreds of millions of years. The later breakthroughs occur only centuries apart.

The sequence for Chart 4 is roughly as follows:

1. The first atoms emerge.
2. Atoms coalesce to form the first molecules of matter.
3. Molecules of matter coalesce to form giant mother stars and galaxies.
4. The first suns explode seeding the universe with the raw materials for new stars, solar systems, and life.
5. Galaxies seed billions of suns and planets.
6. One-celled organisms begin to evolve in Earth's oceans.
7. Multicellular life forms divide and diversify.
8. Primitive plant and animal species move out of the oceans to evolve on Earth's land masses.
9. Breakthrough of sexual reproduction begins a new era of animal and plant diversity.

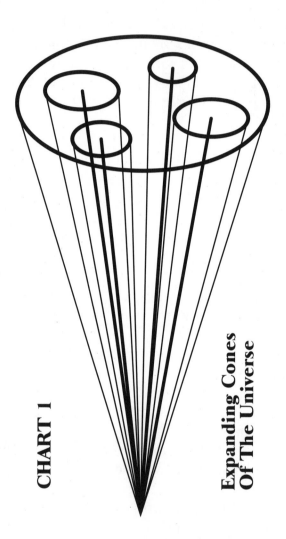

CHART 1

**Expanding Cones
Of The Universe**

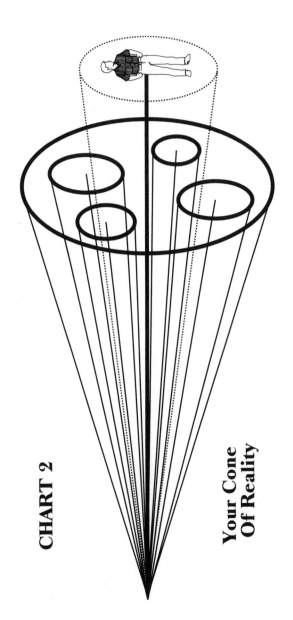

CHART 2

Your Cone Of Reality

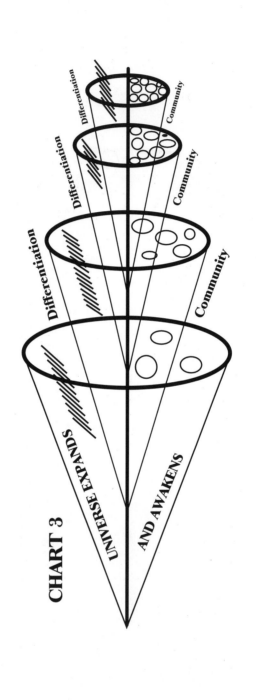

CHART 3

UNIVERSE EXPANDS

AND AWAKENS

Differentiation

Differentiation

Differentiation

Community

Community

Community

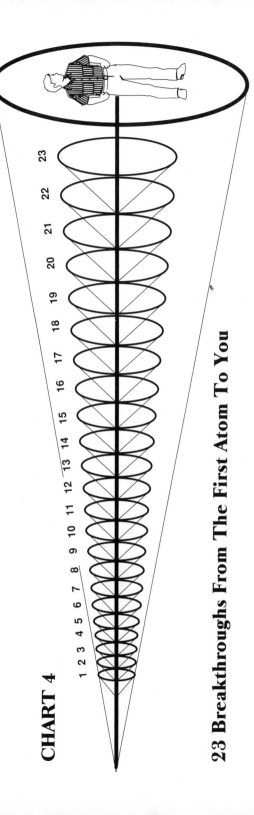

CHART 4

1 2 3 4 5 6 7 8 9 10 11 12 13 14 15 16 17 18 19 20 21 22 23

23 Breakthroughs From The First Atom To You

10. Millions of new life experiments are launched by recombining DNA.
11. Dinosaurs disappear and the Cenozoic Age of mammals and   flowers begins.
12. Sixty-five million years of preparation transforms Earth into a magnificent garden planet.
13. First experiments in consciousness end with the extinction of the Neanderthals.
14. *Homo sapiens* survive through creative co-existence with other life communities of Earth.
15. First unfolding of consciousness is one of unity with nature.
16. Second unfolding of consciousness awakens to a separate spirit world in nature; a world of goddesses with powers of fertility; a world of birth, death, and rebirth cycles.
17. Third unfolding of consciousness awakens to many competing gods, each with human characteristics: jealous, demanding, unpredictable in behavior.
18. Fourth unfolding of consciousness awakens to a sacred, structured relationship among the world of nature, humans, and divinities in one Great Chain of Being.
19. Fifth unfolding of consciousness awakens to divinity of one God: God as stern law giver, humans are separated from the Chain of Being and given dominion over nature.
20. Sixth unfolding of consciousness awakens to divinity as a God of love, compassion, and justice; humans are called to transcend the physical world; matter and spirit are polarized.
21. Seventh unfolding of consciousness awakens to a transformed cosmos; a round Earth circles the

sun; first Western scientists describe a clockwork universe, a universe created by a God who then withdrew, leaving humans in charge.

22. Eighth unfolding of consciousness awakens to a desacralized universe with all divinity withdrawn, humans totally in control, and all mystery explainable by science; existential meaning exists only in the eye of the beholder; the "journey" of the universe is seen as the result of mindless, accidental events with no intrinsic purpose or direction.

23. The ninth unfolding of consciousness awakens to a new empirical story in which science and mystery coexist and embrace each other; the sacred is back; human meaning and purpose are back; hubris (unwarranted pride) is gone; all levels of consciousness are seen as containing vital truths; all are essential but partial revelations in an unfolding process that is at a new breakthrough point now, and that will continue into the future.

Miriam MacGillis concludes that there are no accidents in the unfolding process of the universe, just as there are no accidents in the unfolding process of our own lives. There are no accidents, but many surprises. There are also dead ends, experiments that work, and experiments that don't. At the human level, only experiments bonded by the "gravity" of love succeed in the long run. When a civilization takes a wrong turn, takes its agenda into its own hands (or heads), communion is broken.

ISLANDS OF MOMENTARY CLARITY

Ben, I agree with you that charts are useful tools for visualizing reality. My only caution is that charts, graphs, tables, and maps can seem so conclusive. In academic settings, they are used to put an end to discussions. They should be used, I think, as discussion starters. They are needed as navigational aids and synthesizers. I think of them as little islands we can retreat to when sailing through intellectual storms — islands of momentary clarity. The important thing to remember is that reality is much more complex than anything we can put on paper.

I think the tragedy of those of us who teach in colleges and universities is that we live in an island world. Each discipline cultivates its own little archipelago. It's a lonely life. We natives read the travel literature and write about the beauty of our little bit of academic turf. We seldom share with each other our personal journeys.

Students are ferried back and forth from island to island. They are treated to moments of clarity here and there. They are recruited by island head hunters to major in whatever one archipelago or another has to offer. They are assured that over on the mainland there will be jobs waiting for them. If they had illusions that there was more to life than a ferryboat education leading to a job, they are taught to forget them forthwith.

NEW ENDINGS AND NEW BEGINNINGS

At times of major awakenings, as is happening now, there is an experience of new beginnings, but also an awareness that something old and familiar is passing away. I see the endings as nevertheless providing their own contributions to the ongoing process. The dinosaurs disappeared 65 million years ago, but their contributions from the previous 150 million years did not. The beat goes on, so to speak. Chart 5, which shows the transformative process of endings and beginnings, is an attempt to follow the beat. What significant endowments of past breakthroughs are now being synthesized, composted, and transformed through the funnel of this new awakening?[3]

WHAT IS ENDING/BEING TRANSFORMED?

1. What is ending is the 65 million-year geological time period we call the Cenozoic Age. Science and technology have at present become powerful enough to transform the geology, climate, and life systems of the planet, but in the future, as Thomas Berry tells us,

   - No life form, not even a blade of grass, will survive on Earth unless it is accepted and fostered by the human.
   - For humanity to survive it must redefine what it means to be human, so that we can reinhabit Earth as contributing members of Earth's community.
   - We will need to see Earth's community no longer as a collection of objects for our use, but as subjects with both rights and a sacred claim to habitat that is equal to our own.

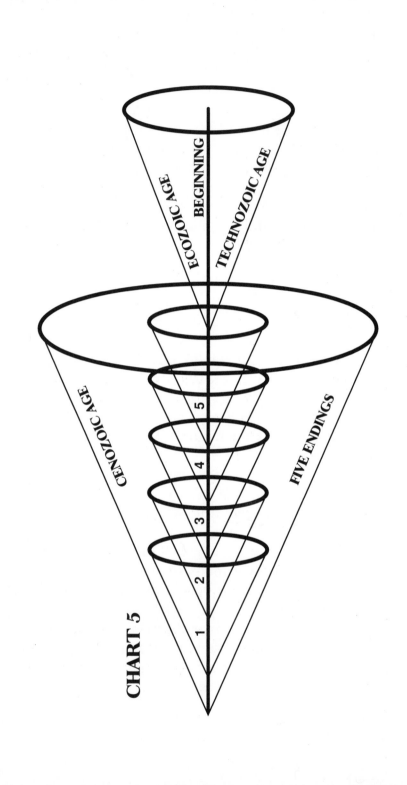

CHART 5

ECOZOIC AGE

BEGINNING

TECHNOZOIC AGE

CENOZOIC AGE

FIVE ENDINGS

1 2 3 4 5

2. At the end of the Cenozoic Age, the anthropomorphic worldview of despiritualized science, and the assumption that it is an adequate guide for human behavior, is being transformed. Mystery, awe, and a sense of the sacred will be essential ingredients, along with "critical thinking" for problem-solving and future planning.

3. Also being transformed are our self-assertive, "value-free" assumptions that dominate economic and political institutions in our industrialized world. Survival will require a synthesis of these along with integrative, ecological, spiritual values.

4. The specialized, discipline-based, segmented, archipelago style of teaching that dominates educational institutions is similarly being transformed. To bridge these island kingdoms of academia will require a new focus on "learning" rather than on "teaching," and on interdisciplinary problem-solving rather than on subject-content memorization. Educational objectives must be concerned with "being," as well as "knowing." They must also focus on compassion for, as well as classification of, the world we observe.

5. Finally, our models of human progress and success are undergoing transformation. In the past, these were seen as the natural outcomes of competition, domination, consumption, efficiency, and constantly increasing productivity. Values that must be included in the new progress-success equation include aesthetics, personal satisfaction, meaning, sustainability, interdependence, and congruence.

"Survival of the fittest" must be reinterpreted to better understand Darwin's intent; fitness is less a matter of being the toughest, most competitive and aggressive species, and more a matter of fitting in, cooperation, interdependence, and contribution to the vitality of the biotic community.

WHAT IS BEGINNING?

From the perspective of Earth Literacy, the most important question that humans face is: What new geologic period will replace the Cenozoic Age? Thomas Berry believes there are two possibilities: the Ecozoic Age, on the one hand, and the Technozoic Age, on the other. What will transpire is a matter of human will at this point.

1. If we move into an Ecozoic Age, there will be no human "progress" understood apart from Earth progress. We will recognize that there can be no human health if Earth is not healthy. We will see Earth as primary and humankind as derivative. The human economy will function in relationship to the Earth economy. Human politics, law, and education will be rooted in the same processes that have characterized Earth for the last four billion years. We will see ourselves as participants in the unfolding universe story. We will honor diversity and community everywhere. We will seek in our own deep interiority the wisdom and guidance needed in order for our lives to make sense and have meaning in the new Ecozoic Age.

2. If we move into the Technozoic Age, we will continue to treat the Earth community as a collection of objects for our use. We will step up efforts to fix Earth's mechanical problems. We will use every means at our disposal to redesign the planet to our liking. We will see Earth as a temporary space platform, a place to perfect our technology. After a while, we will move into outer space on new missions of conquest. Or, Earth may simply heal herself from the cancerous cell that is decimating her community of life and threatening the cosmos with even more destruction.

NOTES

1. This description by Thomas Berry of "The Great Work" is from "Guidelines for Meetings" for The Ecozoic Society, 214 Westgreen Drive, Chapel Hill, NC 27516.

2. Comments made by Miriam Therese MacGillis at a conference sponsored by the Institute for Environmental Ethics, Wolfson Campus, Miami-Dade Community College. The Institute provides Earth Literacy training for faculty who develop modules incorporating concepts of environmental ethics for use in their classrooms. The long-range goals of the campus include teaching "Earth Literacy Across the Curriculum." The Institute sends Earth Literacy student interns to study at the Narrow Ridge Center in Washburn, Tennessee, and faculty to study at Genesis Farm in New Jersey. It also sponsors an Urban Ecology interdisciplinary program and produces a

newsletter. For information write: Institute for Environmental Ethics, MDCC Wolfson Campus, 300 N 2nd Ave., Miami, FL 33132.

3. Another "awakening" is adding a significant new dimension to the Grandmothers' 100-Million-Year Business Report and to the 15-billion-year "new story" of science. It is described in Gil Bailie's recent book, *Violence Unveiled: Humanity at the Crossroads* (New York: Crossroad, 1995). Miriam introduced me to Thomas Berry's insights into geological and cosmological history, but she also introduced me to Gil Bailie's far-reaching insights into history on a spiritual and human scale. Berry shows how a geological age is coming to an end. Bailie shows how a cultural age is coming to an end. Berry demonstrates how, by revisioning the discoveries of our great scientific pioneers, we can come to an understanding of the role of the human in the material world of space, time and matter. Building on the work of anthropologist René Girard, Bailie shows how, by revisioning the discoveries of our great spiritual pioneers, we can come to a new understanding of the role of humans in the non-material world of culture and religion. The focus of *Now That You Know* on the work of the Council of the Grandmothers and my subsequent conversations with Ben do not provide an adequate format for attempting a needed synthesis of Berry's work and Bailie's work. Such a synthesis will be attempted as the next project of the Earth Literacy Communion. For resources on the work of Bailie and Girard, contact The Florilegia Institute, P.O. Box 925, Sonoma, CA 95476-0925.

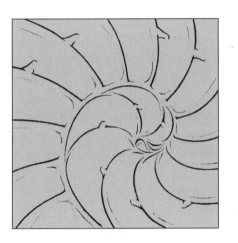

I am done with great things and big things and great institutions and big successes, and I am for those tiny invisible molecular moral forces that work from individual to individual, creeping through the crannies of the world like so many rootlets or like the capillary oozing water, yet which, if you give them time, will bend the hardest monuments of human pride.

William James
The Letters of William James[1]

7

A COW'S OTHER STOMACH

Ben, *Cone Charts* 6 and 7 deal with special concerns of Earth Literacy. They are tools to help students apply the empirical creation story of science to their own lives. The charts apply both Berry's model and the Grandmothers' model of reality to practical tasks students should undertake, tasks like observing the way their society's sound track constantly redirects their life story, or the way education narrows their vision and creates blinders that screen out much of reality. The *Cone Charts* seek to give students a perspective big enough that they will see meaning in their own lives, and hope in their future.

Each breakthrough in human consciousness was preceded first by breakthroughs in perspective, then in breakthroughs in perception. When humans made the first photograph of Earth from outer space, our perspective changed, but our perceptions didn't. Our reality changed, but the way we thought about reality didn't. Looking back on our story, we can see why: our personal security too often depends on maintaining accepted versions of reality. We don't want to rock the boat.

Centuries ago Galileo couldn't show the authorities of his day a photograph of Earth from outer space, but he could show them that Earth was not flat, and that the universe did not revolve around our planet. They could see all of this if they simply looked through his telescope. But they wouldn't look. The change in perception was too threatening.

Every institution in society is a bricks-and-mortar, laws-and-prohibitions expression of perceptions about reality. Government, the stock market, graduate school, kindergarten, hospitals, sewer systems, prisons, electrical grids, advertising, TV religion, newscasters, the drug culture, state lotteries, baby boomers, marriage and divorce, armies, police departments, the homeless are all differentiated parts of a social community grounded on a belief in the way things are. "The way things are" seems perfectly logical based on a past perspective of reality. It was the best humans could imagine at some earlier glorious awakening.

ABSTRACT PERCEPTION

In an abstract way we know all of this. We can even talk about it on our safe little islands of abstraction. This is one of the services the archipelago system of education provides the mainland world of business and politics. Creative young minds can flirt with opposing views of reality without making serious waves. After enough ferrying back and forth, the creativity is worn off. Young minds are thus confined to "tried-and-true" ways of thinking, even though institutions based on such ways of thinking are clearly self-destructive.

Once I received an award from the League of Innovation for engendering "critical thinking" in students about environmental issues. I then was asked to lead a workshop on critical thinking for teachers around the U.S. In the workshop I proposed that critical thinking, as taught on the island kingdoms of academia, perpetuates an "old manner of thinking" that is leading to catastrophe.

One concept I used that many teachers related to was that we were "vaccinating students," especially good students, the ones most likely to take back to the mainland ideas dangerous to the reigning belief system. In the workshop, we agreed that these ideas were like viruses. To guard against them, it was important for students to be inoculated while still on the islands.

I suggested that often the best teachers do the best job of inoculating students. They present the clearest bits and pieces of truth. But these bits of truth, when seen in an educational context that is fragmented and irrelevant, operate in the same way dead viruses do. Dead-virus teaching excites students just enough to stimulate their immune system, but the fever of excitement is contained because the virus is dead. By the time students begin their careers on the mainland, they are safely inoculated against ever taking a live virus-truth seriously.

The trance that allows us to see so much, yet be oblivious to what matters most, is not the result of a sinister plot. The captains of commerce on the mainland and the chief academicians on the islands do their duty as they see it. There are no villains whose elimination will change anything. What must change is not what we see, but the act (or art) of seeing itself.

Education inoculates students so that they will see only one particular reality. It is not an abstract reality. It is the reality of national institutions on which each society depends, and which we ourselves depend. Yet, once we look at a photograph of Earth from outer space, we see the absurdity of institutions that divide the planet into artificial political boundaries.

THE "PRACTICE OF FREEDOM"

Computer-enhanced photos taken from space shuttles show a cancer-like sickness spreading around the planet. College students see these pictures and study the hows and whys of Earth's sickness. Then, eyes unblinking, they graduate into the tenuous world of business-as-usual. Sustainable or not, that is the world they depend on, and they know it.

There is nothing new here. Paulo Freire makes a similar observation in the introduction to his book, *Pedagogy of the Oppressed*:

> There is no such thing as a neutral educational process. Education either functions as an instrument which is used to facilitate the integration of the younger generation into the logic of the present system and bring about conformity to it, or it becomes the "practice of freedom," the means by which people learn to deal collectively and critically with their world.
>
> The development of an educational methodology that facilitates [the "practice of freedom"] will inevitably lead to tension and conflict with a society. But it could also contribute to the formation of a new humanity and mark the beginning of a new era.[2]

Cone Chart 6 provides a perceptual grid for beginning the intricate steps toward a "practice of freedom." It attempts to understand the logic of the present, while escaping its bonds of conformity. It is a continuation of the universe story begun in the previous five charts.

To make a model for this *Cone Chart,* tape two drinking straws together end to end to create a long hollow tube. Slide one end of a straw through the center of a large paper cone. Slide the opposite end of the straw through the center of a smaller paper cone. You should now have two cones pierced by the straw, each facing the same direction.

Cone 1, the larger, represents the creation and outward expansion of the universe. It is the time/ space reality in which you are located. For 15 billion years the unfolding of innumerable breakthroughs within this sphere has led to the creative possibilities now present in you.

Cone 2, the smaller, represents your life. It begins with your conception in your mother's womb. Take time to think about your awakening into life as another breakthrough in the creation story. The external shell of the straw tube is like an umbilical cord linking you with the beginning of creation, in many ways feeding the very identity of the person who is reading this now. It is your connection to all past breakthroughs. To make this image concrete, mark on your straw all the awakenings recorded on Chart 4. Read the description of each aloud. This is but a tiny catalog of the billions of steps in the creation process that have coalesced in your personal awak-

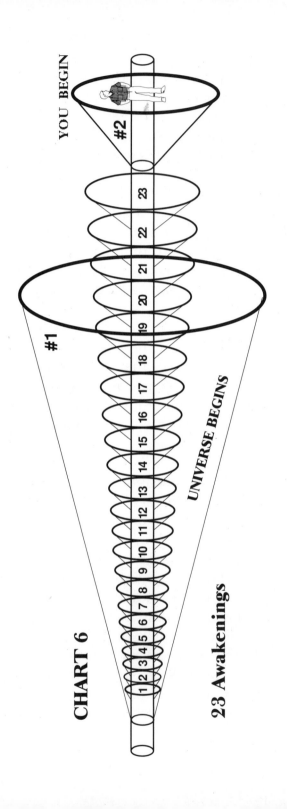

CHART 6

YOU BEGIN

#2

#1

UNIVERSE BEGINS

23 Awakenings

1 2 3 4 5 6 7 8 9 10 11 12 13 14 15 16 17 18 19 20 21 22 23

ening. Each was needed to bring into existence the possibilities that you represent.

The marks on the straw link you through space and time with events and awakenings that have a physical beginning. The interior of the straw represents a reality outside the dimensions of time and space. It is the immeasurable "place within" from which you can view a reality without horizons. Only astronauts can go into outer space and look back, but each of us can go into our own inner space and see from whence we came.

To do this, you need not "go" anywhere. This is the message of the hollow straw. You carry within you a perspective from which you can see the whole and experience all awakenings as one. Within this deep well of your own unconscious all the ambiguity and paradox of surface-living fade. All of the differentiated members of the Earth community -- even those you fear or who fear you -- are seen as essential. Go deep enough and you will see that every spiritual tradition that has ever existed was essential. All dissolve into the same single pinprick of light that emerged over 15 billion years ago from an unknown, and unknowable, mysterious source.

You can choose whatever name for this that feels right to you. You can decide for yourself whether or not it is real. Every awakening of human consciousness shown on Chart 4, except the desacralized eighth consciousness, held this inner perspective to be the most real, something to be cultivated. Humans have called that inner place by many names -- soul, spirit, intelligence, force-field, implicate order, the One, Brahman, Nirvana, The Great Spirit, etc.

In using *Cone Chart 6*, it is important not to get bogged down with labels. Ben, you said your classmates didn't think the world they were being prepared for was real, that they were being hooked on a game that didn't make sense. When we talked, you asked how I knew if any of this was real. The purpose of charts 6 and 7 is for making sense out of life, for determining what is real.

NEW POSSIBILITIES FOR PERCEIVING REALITY

Cone Chart 7 is an enlargement of the cone of reality that represents your lifetime in the previous diagram. It extends from your conception to the present moment. During your lifetime you will experience many personal awakenings — physical awakenings, emotional awakenings, intellectual awakenings, spiritual awakenings.

The four small cones in chart 7 represent significant watersheds in your lifetime, each signifying a change in perspective, a time when something shifts in your life. With each shift, new possibilities for perceiving reality open.

Cone 1 teaches that shifts in perception occur even in the womb. They are triggered by chemical signals and genetically programmed molecular switches. At each shift, your developing body responds in new ways. You sense your environment in a new manner — a new burst of differentiation occurs. Cells divide into communities of cells. Atoms coalesce into communities of atoms. Communities of cells become the community of your body: tissue, bone, heart, lungs, limbs, eyes, brain cells. From conception, you continue the ancient beat of creation, and the ancient beat continues in you.

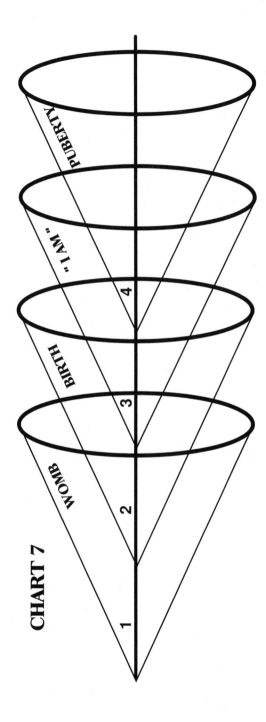

CHART 7

WOMB

BIRTH

"I AM"

PUBERTY

1
2
3
4

The Ancient Beat Of Creation Continues Through You

Cone 2 teaches that at birth your perspective changes radically. A new kind of differentiation begins. New perceptions create and recreate the reality you experience while growing up. Without ever thinking about what you are doing, you perceive the world of language, of balance and motion, music and color, love and fear. As in humankind's earliest consciousness, you experience these different realities in yourself. You do not differentiate yourself from the world around you, however. You are, in earliest childhood, still one with the universe. You are the universe experiencing itself.

Cone 3 teaches that about the time when you start school your separateness sinks in. A new awakening begins. You are able to experience not simply "I want" and "I feel," but the clear certainty that "I am." From this new perspective, the world seems to divide again. You not only perceive yourself as separate from everything else, but you can perceive your thoughts as separate from yourself as well. Soon, thinking will become abstract. It is possible to continue this process of differentiating ideas and experiences for the rest of your life. If you do continue, if you get this far on your journey, you will know what is real. Long before that you will know whether or not you are living a life that makes sense.

Cone 4 teaches that you have the possibility of becoming more than you ever imagined. Just when, as a youth, you think you have a handle on reality, a new perspective pulls the rug out from under your feet. It is commonly known as puberty. Ancient molecular switches, programmed in relatives long extinct, go into action. The hormones that revolutionize your body also change the way you perceive reality.

Two mysterious forces take hold of your imagination. Two voids open up that will haunt you for the rest of your life. One is the void of sex. The other is the void of meaning. They are related. At about the same time you feel your first sexual yearnings, something else deep inside you beckons. Now that you know yourself as separate, questions arise. Who are you? What are you supposed to do with your life? Why are you here?

You are a member of the only species that is burdened by such questions. Other beings in the animal and plant world are equipped with additional molecular switches that are missing in you. These switches tell elephants how to be elephants, eagles how to be eagles, salmon how to be salmon, microbes how to be microbes, and dogs how to be dogs.

Because your dog cannot think "I am," it doesn't have to ask questions to find meaning in its life. His life is his meaning. He does not experience separation between life and death. Once you think "I am," the shadow thought, "someday I won't be" is not far behind. The culture you live in does not include shadow thoughts in its bricks and mortar, business-as-usual reality. The politics and economics of business-as-usual are premised on the belief that the universe is going nowhere. Therefore, neither are you, except as a trustworthy cog in the business machine, except as a trustworthy consumer. No one who has thought "I am" and "someday I won't be" would buy into such a reality if he or she weren't first inoculated with dead viruses from society's sound track.[3]

Ben, you can see that the archipelago institutions of education have their work cut out for them. To a large degree, educational institutions are abetted by religious institutions in derailing the powerful impulses turned loose at puberty, i.e., the longing to know one's identity and to identify with another human being, to know one's meaning and to identify with the source of that meaning, to know where the universe is going and to go wherever its journey takes you.

Chart 7 ends with the cone of puberty. In one's lifetime, there are many more awakenings: a cone for graduating from high school, going to work, entering college, more graduations, getting married, the birth of a child, the death of loved ones, perhaps a personal near-death experience.

An Earth Literacy study plan can be outlined by using a *Cone Chart*. All learning experiences can be pictured and related to each other in a time/space cone. The cone can show a semester's work, or longer or shorter periods of time. The resulting "perceptual grid" is similar to a process developed by physicist Peter Russell called "mind mapping."[4]

In many ways, the *Cone Charts* in a perceptual grid function like a "cow's other stomach." The cones do the work of the rumen in ruminant, or cud-chewing, animals. As ruminants browse, food moves into a stomach designed for the temporary storage of cud. This is the stomach called a rumen. Later, the cud is retrieved and chewed leisurely before digestion begins.

In Earth Literacy, learning is considered more of a browsing activity than a cataloging one. New information, new experiences are like the cud a cow stores in her other stomach. Before anything is neatly pigeonholed in standard academic fashion, it is chewed leisurely, over and over. Out of this process, unexpected connections are discovered — a new insight, a new relationship, and, occasionally, an "Aha!" that can reshape your whole map of knowing.

Ben, you asked for charts. You wanted something visual you could use to critique what is happening around you. You wanted a tool to help identify what is disabling you and what is enabling you to live. Are the charts helpful? Let's talk again.

• • •

I looked for Ben, and when I saw him he was standing by a window. I had the impression he was looking across a peaceful meadow. There were cows grazing. He pointed outside.

"In chart six, you referred to the 'practice of freedom,'" *he said. "Those cows are enclosed in a fence. The owner of the cows can decide if they live or die. Yet, I see them engaged in a 'practice of freedom' that I envy. It's a good example for me to see. Cows being so leisurely at doing precisely what their life work is about. Chewing and storing cud. Digesting and assimilating the chemistry of Earth into their bodies.*

"I like the cow's other stomach idea. It will be helpful to me. But there's still something missing from the picture. If the human is the species in whom Earth is awakening, what's the game about? Why wouldn't we want to go where the universe is going? Like everything else is doing."

Ben turned to face me, and the scene out the window faded from view.

"No other species," I said, "makes a choice to go where the universe is going. It goes. Choice is what makes humans unique. We have a choice in the matter. We can say 'yes,' 'maybe,' or 'no.'

"But most of us don't know what we really want. We think we want what society's sound track tells us to want. Ben, you were an exception. You could teach the Grandmothers and me because somehow your inoculation didn't take."

"I don't feel like an exception," Ben said. "I'd like to feel as confident and content as cows chewing their cud.

"If humans are a part of something bigger than themselves, something that's trying to unfold, how could they block it? Why would they? There's still a big piece missing from the puzzle."

We sat for a while facing each other. Ben's frustration was plain to see.

"You are right," I said. "The puzzle isn't complete. Let me try to complete the picture. At least sketch out pieces we need to work on.

"I will do what the Grandmothers did. I'll consult some authorities I have faith in, ask them what they think is needed to complete the puzzle. Are you with me?"

"I'm with you," Ben said with a grin.

NOTES

1. William James to Henry James, May 4, 1907, in *The Letters of William James*, 2 vols. (Boston: The Atlantic Monthly Press, 1920) 2 : 277.

2. Paulo Freire, *Pedagogy of the Oppressed* (New York: Seabury Press, 1970) xii.

3. The economics of business-as-usual is being revisioned in more realistic terms on several fronts. The following are two attempts to plan for a "soft landing" at the end of the current Cenozoic geological era.

- Decades of work as a "change agent" have led economist Robert Theobald to create two successful grassroots movements. I have been privileged to participate in both the Action Linkage Network and the Many-to-Many dialogue exchange groups. While I have subscribed to dozens of well-edited professional journals, the only publication I read the moment it arrives at my door is the pasted-together, photocopied M-2-Ms of the AL Network. I believe that Theobald tapped the richest vein of creativity in existence when he recruited amateurs to volunteer to do the pasting and copying, and ordinary folks like me to begin exchanging ideas. To obtain a sample issue of the M-2-M, write to Bill Holden, Editor, Cooperatives and Community M-2-M, P.O. Box 1692, Bellflower, CA 90707-1692. For an introduction to the work of Robert Theobald, see Turning of the Century: Personal and Organizational Strategies for Your Changed World (Indianapolis: Knowledge Systems, 1992).

- The most sophisticated revisioning effort of business-as-usual that I know of is the Institute of Noetic Science's new PATHFINDING: A Collaborative Inquiry Project. This is a worldwide effort initiated by the late Willis W. Harman and Thomas J. Hurley. The starting point of the dialogues is the Main Question as follows:

What is the central purpose of industrialized societies when it no longer makes sense for that central purpose to be economic production, when production... does not lead to a viable future, but does lead to: systematic destruction of natural resources; systematic destruction of community; systematic transfer of wealth upwards; systematic marginalization of persons, communities, and cultures; systematic erosion and denial of the sense of the spiritual or sacred; systematic creation of learned incapacity and helplessness?

The urgency given by the Institute for Noetic Sciences for addressing the Main Question is exactly the same urgency the Council of Grandmothers felt when they decided that "enough is enough!" The urgency for the PATHFINDING project is that "the entire way of life of the modern world is not sustainable on a finite planet in the long term. It makes little difference whether by 'long term' we mean half a century or two centuries.... Nothing short of fundamental transformation of all our powerful institutions and, underlying that, of modern thought and prejudice will alter the ultimate reckoning."

To receive an Invitation to Participate, a Progress Report, and a Draft Scenario 1.0 (viewed from the perspective of the year 2000), write INS, 475 Gate 5 Rd., Suite 300, Sausalito, CA 94965; e-mail: thurley@well.com.

4. Peter Russell's works include *Brain Book* (Palo Alto, CA: Global Brain, Inc., 1984), *The Global Brain Awakens: Our Next Evolutionary Leap* (Palo Alto, CA: Global Brain, Inc., 1995), and *The White Hole in Time* (San Francisco: HarperSanFrancisco, 1995).

The window in time that opened when life on Earth took the leap into Homo Sapiens is at the point of closing. We are in the last moments of our 50,000 year dash from emerging consciousness to full enlightenment. We are in a race against time itself.

It is we alive today who have the responsibility of guiding this species on. It is we who have to find ways to release ourselves from this self-centered phase of our development and open ourselves to the full significance of the timeless moment — and to the full significance of the present time.

Peter Russell
The White Hole in Time[1]

8

TWO WAYS TO COMPLETE THE PUZZLE

Ben, in this chapter I will consult two authorities I respect, Thomas Berry and Helen Wallace, and attempt to put together a thumbnail sketch of how I think each might answer your questions: What is missing from the puzzle? Why don't humans choose to go where the universe is going?

THOMAS BERRY'S FIVE-PART CRITIQUE OF THE PUZZLE[2]

In a series of lectures entitled "The Human Presence Within the Earth Community," Thomas Berry encourages young people to critique the world in which they find themselves. Each item in his personal critique can be seen as a piece of the puzzle that has been given to us to assemble. Once we are able to see the picture clearly, we can begin to ascertain what is both enabling and disabling our lives.

Critique 1: We Are Autistic

Berry believes that we who live in industrial societies have become, in a manner of speaking, autistic, i.e., emotionally cut off from the natural world. We are pathologically removed from our deep psychic link to Earth and the universe. We no longer hear the voices of the other beings with whom we share the planet. Sadly, both education and religion are failing to deal with this profound cultural denial.

When we teach about human society apart from Earth society, we teach an absurdity. We create dangerous abstractions and leave students devoid of spiritual sensitivity. Because education and religion have been incompetent to the task before them, the planet has been degraded, and humans have lost touch with their ground of being.

Critique 2: We Are Chosen

None of us chose to be born in this time of immense responsibility, but we have been chosen by the universe. We have been chosen through a sequence of multiform, celebratory events. The birth of each of us, like the birth of a star, is such an event.

If we are awake to our origins, if we rethink our situation, if we are clear regarding our objective, we can do magnificent things. We can stop giving trivial answers to complex questions. We can end our plundering process. It is the nature of the universe that it supply the needs of the moment, and it is supplying those needs right now.

Critique 3: We Have Lost Our Story

The essence of the universe is celebration. The first awakening of the human psyche required a world of flowers, of bird song and exquisite beauty. Beauty is needed to celebrate the divine story because it helps ease the inevitable pain that accompanies awakening consciousness. This is why it has been, and still is, important for all people in all cultures to understand their story, to understand who they are and how their world came into being.

The universe story is primary, but religious ritual and celebration are needed to reveal how our individual stories and the universe story are intertwined. They are also needed to reveal the divine and to orient us with the energy, serenity, and sagacity needed to enter the future. When people lose their story they become disoriented. They lose their inner poise and enter into strange pathologies.

Critique 4: We Are Totally Unprepared

We are plunging into an irreversible shift of enormous proportions, and we are unprepared for what we are doing. The shift is a change in our relationship with the natural world. As we come to the end of the Cenozoic Age, we have begun to shift Earth from automatic to manual control. Earth will never function the same way. Whether the new age will be Technozoic or Ecozoic is now up to us.

In the past, Earth performed its magic quite well without a human presence. Life was then encompassed by the natural world, but now the natural world is encompassed by the human. This is an enormous shift of balance and an unprecedented responsibility. Human technologies must now become coherent with Earth technologies. Our plunder can no longer be called "progress" — human survival depends on correcting this nefarious distortion of truth.

To correct this distortion, our academic and professional disciplines will need to be reoriented. The first concern of economics will have to be the preservation of the Earth economy. The first concern of medicine must become the health of the planet. In the legal sphere, the rights of species to a livable habitat will need to be addressed, and linguists will have to devise an Ecozoic language that recognizes and illuminates our cultural pathology. Ethicists will have to name and address the absolute evils of biocide and genocide, and the first concern of philosophy will need to be an understanding of Earth, not as a collection of objects for human use, but as a communion of intrinsically valuable subjects.

Critique 5: "Democracy" is a Conspiracy

Our democratic institutions only serve to foster a conspiracy of humans against the natural world. Universities and religious establishments engender attitudes that glorify the human and devastate the planet. Our democratic institutions provide little guidance, little self-critique, and do nothing to awaken us to our real situation. We live unaware of the sacred community in which we participate.

We need new spiritual sensitivities to the presence of the divine in all of Earth's subjects. To do the ten thousand things that need to be done is not enough; the Technozoic mindset cannot create a viable human society. "Sustainable development" is not enough, nor is "fixing the environment."

An Ecozoic agenda for Earth-literate citizens will mean an end to human plunder. It will mean living in the ambivalence of mystery, celebrating the story of the universe, and honoring the affection the story engenders in human hearts.

HELEN WALLACE'S SIX-PART INVISIBLE PRISON PUZZLE

Ben, keep in mind what Thomas Berry has said as I recall six concepts from the files of the Council of Grandmothers. Helen Wallace was a master of paradox. She had the ability to entertain simultaneously two seemingly contradictory positions. She believed that the same empirical science that had locked the prison door of our minds could also be used to gain our freedom.

The best way to free ourselves from our chains, she used to say, is not by "breaking out," but by "breaking in." The first five of the following concepts are based on modern scientific studies that Helen presented to the Council of Grandmothers. She called each a "break-in" breakthrough. Each makes the invisible prison a little more visible. Each helps us achieve a better understanding of who we are by first helping us to understand who and what we are not.

The sixth concept Helen presented was about a 5,000 year old philosophy from India which she thought could teach us to apply insights from modern brain research to today's most pressing human problems.

Think about each of these concepts, Ben, and let me know if they clarify the big picture for you.

Concept 1: Brains that Cannot Communicate

Teachers often tell us that at the most we use only 10 to 15% of our brains, the assumption being that if we were to use more of our mental muscle we would be smarter and the world would be a better place. We do not use too little of our brain, Helen used to say; our problem is that we use too much of our wrong brain.

Helen got this idea from Dr. Paul MacLean, chief of the Laboratory of Brain Evolution and Behavior at the

U.S. National Institute of Mental Health.[3] According to MacLean, we all come equipped with not one but three brains. Two we inherited from pre-human times: the first is a pea-sized, reptilian brain covered over by a second, ping-pong ball-sized ancient mammalian brain. These artifacts of human consciousness operate on entirely different principles from the grapefruit-sized human forebrain we now possess.

Based on his research, Maclean believes that one of humankind's greatest problems is that a communication gap exists between our ancient brains and our modern one. Whenever we feel threatened, our old brains get our attention first. That's what they were designed for: fight or flight. The creativity and long-range thinking of our human brain would be useless to wild creatures like crocodiles and horses whose "thinking" is limited to primitive survival skills like guarding a territory, protecting possessions, competing for status, organizing the herd, knowing who is top dog, and outfoxing the enemy.

Unfortunately, MacLean says, these are the skills most in demand in the world we are taught to believe is real. That is why almost all the creativity utilized by our all-human forebrain is used to carry out projects cooked up by our reptilian and mammalian brains. This may explain why we are so enamored with nuclear bombs, why we are depleting Earth's resources to appease our voracious appetites, and why we have killed more than 100 million members of our own species in the twentieth century.

Concept 2: Seeing Like Half-blind Cats

Helen believed that a cat experiment done at Stanford University, and replicated in other laboratories around the country, gives us a glimpse of the kind of invisible prison that humans create for themselves. The purpose of the cat experiment was to observe how the brain creates its own reality. A litter of kittens was divided into two groups before their eyes were opened. Each group was raised under identical enclosures, save for one variable: the walls of one were covered with vertical stripes, while the walls of the other had horizontal stripes. Each enclosure was kept dark all but a few hours every day.

As the kittens grew, the two groups learned to see two entirely different realities, each a result of the visual cues received from their environment. When set free in a normal room, one group of cats could gracefully jump over chair rungs, but they would run blindly into chair legs. Their brains did not "see" a vertical reality. The other group of cats could easily negotiate chair legs, but chair rungs posed a real problem. Their brains did not "see" a horizontal reality.

Helen's point was that the reality we each see is shaped by the "enclosure" in which we were raised — our school, our family, our friends, our work, and our society. In this sense, we are all like half-blind cats. Our brains "see" only the narrow view of reality we learn to observe. If we operate out of our old brains, we will continue to run headlong into circumstances we cannot see, and too often we will deny that they exist. But, Ben, *if* we learn to direct our lives with our human forebrain, our narrow reptilian and mammalian view of reality will be constantly expanded. We will learn to respect realities seen and experienced by others, ones that we do not see now. Our lives, from birth to death, will be a constant adventure.

Concept 3: You Are Not Your Family's Image

One of Helen's favorite psychology experiments involved an exploration of how the emotions of children are shaped. The series of experiments took place in a carpeted laboratory furnished like a living room. A mother sat on a chair and watched her infant crawl on the floor while a psychologist and several graduate students watched through a one-way mirror.

At some point, a hidden observer released a toy robot which marched toward the infant and stopped within reaching distance. A high-speed camera recorded the movement of the infant's eyes so that any momentary glance toward the mother would not be missed. This glance registered an impression in the infant's brain not unlike the brush stroke a painter makes when creating an image on canvas. In this case, however, the image was an impression of the world that this new, little person would soon believe to be real.

In one session of the experiment, the mother was instructed to respond to the infant's glance with an expression of fear. Immediately, the infant drew back and cried. In the following session, another mother was instructed to respond with an expression of trust. That infant reached out and hugged the robot.

Thousands of such glances and unspoken feelings from parents and friends help create the reality we each see and feel. Helen did not suggest that this is the "wrong" way to learn reality, it is merely how all of us learn. But what is important for each of us to know is that our reality is a "painting," not a mirror image of what is there. Even though many people have contributed their brush strokes, it is nevertheless *our* painting. Once we know this, we can pick up the brush and revise, refine, create our own masterpiece. We can also learn to appreciate the masterpieces of others. This, Helen believed, is the lifetime task of each of us, and one we cannot begin too soon.

Concept 4: You Are Not Your Teacher's Image

Helen used to speak of an experiment with "slow learners" in which students were divided into two groups. Group "A" was assigned to one teacher who was told that her students were learning disabled, while Group "B" was assigned to another teacher who was told that her charges were merely "late bloomers." The latter teacher also received a report saying that a well-known psychologist had tested all slow learners in the school and found that her students were actually quite bright and could be expected to "bloom" in the next school period. The difference between these groups did not involve the students, rather it involved the reality that each teacher was given to believe in.

Ben, you can probably guess the result of this experiment. It delighted Helen. The difference in the teacher's picture of reality made a difference in the reality perceived by the students. The teacher who expected her students to bloom did bloom; test scores improved by the end of the term. By contrast, the teacher who expected her students to be slow remained slow with test scores remaining where they had always been.

Helen said that many different experiments on this "self-fulfilling" prophecy phenomenon had been performed, even with animals. In one such experiment, lab technicians were told that they were working with a special breed of smarter mice. Surprisingly, even though the animals were actually ordinary, dull mice, they did run through a maze faster and tested smarter. Again, a hidden camera revealed the probable cause: the technicians gave these mice more time to make decisions in the maze, and they handled them with what appeared to be more respect and care.

Helen's conclusion: to a dangerous degree, the expectations of others shape the "reality" which becomes our "invisible prison," yet neither they nor we perceive the imprisoning process in which we all participate.

Concept 5: You Are Not the Adult You Become

Helen was the only teacher I ever knew who thought the science of neotony was worth talking about. Neotony proposes that the current manner in which children develop into adults is a mistake, for both the children and the human species. Neotony is a real science that has an even more complicated name: paedomorphosis. The perceptions of reality taught by neotony, as you might imagine, do not fit into the reality that we are all taught to believe in.

In his book, *Growing Young*,[4] the British anthropologist Ashley Montagu discusses this field of research. He suggests that if we were to teach the facts of life according to the science of neotony, human survival would be assured for many more centuries. However, we would have completely to change the way we educate our young, and also change our view of what it means to become an adult.

Montagu begins by describing how baby animals go through a "hardening stage" as they become adults. They lose most of the characteristics of their youth: physically, their body proportions change; they go from playful to short-tempered; they become fixed in patterns of behavior; they lose their capacity to adapt.

Unfortunately, Montagu says, many adult humans harden in much the same way, and this is not natural for us. It is not the way nature designed humans to develop. Our hardened view of adulthood results from a dangerous misconception about reality.

When we are children, we are often asked, "What are you going to be when you grow up?" This is the wrong question, says Montagu. We should be asking children, "What are you going to be as you grow young?" This is what it means to be a member of a neotonous species with a big human forebrain: physically and mentally we are designed by nature not to harden into the kind of adults most children know and come to be like. Rather, our heritage, as members of the human species, involves the possibility of developing a perpetually youthful attitude. This inheritance is humankind's most valuable survival trait.

Montagu lists the characteristics humans most need in times of crisis. They are, he says, the very qualities that modern societies systematically train out of their children: curiosity, open-mindedness, playfulness, imagination, a willingness to experiment, flexibility, humor, energy, receptiveness to new ideas, honesty, eagerness to learn. Most valuable of all is the need to give and receive love.

These are the traits, Montagu believes, that helped our ancient ancestors survive while other species did not. Some 300,000 years ago, the behavior of "Swanscombe man and woman" was not locked into unchangeable patterns by a pea-sized or a ping-pong sized brain. "Neanderthal man" had a new, human brain as large as ours, and were as educable as we are.

Helen's conclusion from Montagu's book was that our ancient grandmothers and grandfathers might have been more childlike, and even more fully "human" than we adults are today. They may have used their big human forebrains in ways that humans now have forgotten. The value of playfulness and giving and receiving love would certainly be welcome additions to our current perceptions of what it means to be a responsible human adult.

Concept 6: An Ancient Way to Know Yourself

Helen proposed a theory that the gap between our human forebrain and our two ancient brains makes it easy for society to hook us on a game that has no meaning. She related this theory to concepts taught in India by Ayur Veda philosophers over 5,000 years ago.

Teachers of Ayurveda developed methods of education and medicine to allow children to grow into healthy, open-minded, imaginative adults. They understood how the experiences of childhood shape our beliefs. Ayurvedic training sought to counter two types of beliefs that rob us in childhood of qualities we most need to retain.

The first type of belief is shaped by society's sound track, that persistent background stimulation that inculcates a reality similar to the horizontal and vertical stripes in the half-blind cat experiment. These are beliefs and hidden assumptions communicated by countless unspoken glances between infant and parents, and by facial expressions and body language. These become part of the background music played by the world we live in. Like the sound track in a movie, it directs our emotions and draws us into the drama of life without our even knowing it. Of course, movies did not exist in India 5,000 years ago, but every society throughout history has had its own sound track. Ours creates a desire for status, possessions, territory, and even enemies, for when society can focus attention on "the other," it can make the most meaningless game seem significant.

The second type of belief that robs us of our most valuable qualities is the expectation that we must decide in advance what kind of adult we want to be. Society's "growing up" question has great power — Ayurveda teachers referred to it as a "premature cognitive commitment." We are too often asked to commit ourselves prematurely to a particular view of reality, and this happens all too early in life.

Ancient Ayurveda teachers were the first scientists of neotony. They proposed that rather than pressuring children into making a premature cognitive commitment to growing up, we should be encouraging them to commit to "growing young." The Ayurvedic first line of defense against society's sound track was the practice of silence, sitting and doing nothing, preferably in a quiet natural setting. If we are silent in the presence of a tree, a rock or a pond, we may hear an inner voice break through. When we learn to hear in silence, the next step in Ayurvedic teaching comes naturally - meditation, also referred to as contemplation, prayer, or yoga.

Some scientists like MacLean now say that these spiritual practices are good not only for the soul, but also for the brain. He even suggests that such practices have the power to bridge the gaps among our three brains. He does not mean "bridge" as a metaphor; silence, contemplation, meditation, prayer and yoga have the power to strengthen neural networks. By quieting our external lives, we increase communication among our brains.

MacLean calls the neural bridge across our brain a "path of empathy." The more we feel empathy for each other and for other creatures, the less power society's sound track has in directing our emotions, and the less our ancient brains will exercise control over our thinking and actions.

Helen believed that it was this "gap" that made us uniquely human. The path of empathy is the path of meaning. She thought the gap in our brain was like a black hole in space, that is, a collapsed star with a gravitational field so powerful that everything around it, even light, is drawn into its center. Black holes seem to connect our universe to another mysterious, invisible reality.

Helen thought the gap in our brains connected us to the mysterious, invisible reality of meaning. The purpose of society's sound track is to make us believe that it can fill the black hole in us, to make us believe that we can find meaning by competing and winning, and by possessing more and more things. And since no amount of winning or possessing can give life meaning, we get hooked. Our ancient brains keep us running faithfully on a treadmill toward society's mirage of success.

When we finally bridge our brain gap, Helen said, everything will change. We will know that beating others in competition cannot give life meaning. We will know that possessing more things only addicts us to wanting still more. I believe the inner gravity Helen described as a black hole is the principle of reality Thomas Berry refers to as "interiority." It is a gap, a black hole, that connects each of us to a reality beyond time and space. It connects us to a "knowing" that is endless and ever fulfilling, a "knowing" that Helen knew would make visible the invisible prison walls that each of us creates for ourselves.

• • •

By the time I sat down in my chair, Ben was already sitting opposite me.

"Did you notice," he said, "that all of Berry's critiques were products of the gap in our brains?"

I said I didn't and asked him to explain.

"If MacLean is right," Ben said, "to see the gap in your own brain would be an incredible breakthrough. You could show it in a perceptual grid. The string could divide the space between the human brain and the reptilian and mammalian brains."

Ben bent over and traced a pattern on the floor. He was excited.

"Where do Berry's critiques fit in?" I asked.

"The gap might be the missing piece," he said, as though talking to himself. The notion that we are chosen is an interesting idea. What created the gap? A series of multiform, celebratory events created it. The gap chose us. What makes us autistic and unprepared? The gap. What makes democracy a conspiracy of humans against the natural world? The gap.

"That's where it gets real interesting...."

Ben sat up straight, put his hands in his lap and closed his eyes. I followed his example. When I opened my eyes he was staring at me.

"Why interesting?" I asked.

"What makes us really human," Ben said, "is all three brains. The big human forebrain by itself wouldn't do it. We need our 'crocodile' and 'wild horse' selves. We need the gap. Don't you see?"

I told Ben that I still did not see. Maybe, almost. But not yet.

"You can't have empathy with what you can't experience," he continued, a little impatiently, "The path of empathy *does more than strengthen neurological ties, more than in-crease communication between brains. Empathy makes three brains one. Empathy makes the human one with all creatures of creation, and one with the One who crates the creatures."*

I nodded in agreement. I would have to allow Ben's description of empathy sink in. I thought about how much Helen would have liked taking part in this dialogue. I also thought about how our discussions would soon come to an end.

"I am curious," Ben said, "You talk about being in kindergarten. I have two questions. When do you think you will graduate? And what is the most important lesson you have learned?"

"Interesting questions," I said, "Give me some time to think about them."

NOTES

1. Peter Russell, *The White Hole in Time* (San Francisco: HarperSanFrancisco, 1995), 328.

2. The following is a summary of a lecture series by Thomas Berry entitled "The Human Presence Within the Earth Community." Audio tapes of the series are available from Global Perspectives, P.O. Box 925, Sonoma, CA 95476.

3. The implications of MacLean's triune brain theory are developed in a very readable text by artist and author Frederick Franck, entitled *To Be Human Against All Odds* (Fremont, CA: Asian Humanities Press, 1991.

4. Ashley Montagu, *Growing Young* (New York: McGraw-Hill, 1988).

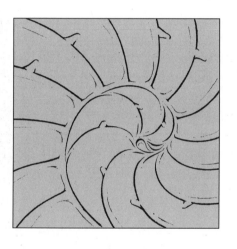

The age of nations has passed. Now, unless we wish to perish we must shake off our old prejudices and build the earth. ...The more scientifically I regard the world, the less I can see any biological future for it except the active consciousness of its unity. Life cannot henceforth advance on our planet... except by breaking down the partitions which still divide human activity and entrusting itself unhesitatingly to faith in the future.

Pierre Teilhard de Chardin
"The Spirit of the Earth"[1]

9

GRADUATING FROM KINDERGARTEN

When Helen Wallace was still alive she conducted a ritual graduation for me. Actually, she planned the graduation because of you, Ben. I will describe it to you, and then I'll address your question about the most important thing I have learned.

In preparation for the ritual, Helen and I completed the last of what she called "the practical things" we did together. We spent a day reading from several of her favorite books and piecing together quotes for a graduation meditation. We looked at Buckminster Fuller's *Critical Path*,[2] Allen Wheelis's *On Not Knowing How to Live*,[3] and *The Saviors of God: Spiritual Exercises* by Nikos Kasantzakis.[4]

Not long before Helen was incapacitated with Alzheimer's, and before Sally Milledge died, I was officially adopted into the Council of Grandmothers. This, they said, was my graduation from kindergarten.

A GRADUATION CEREMONY TO BE DANCED

I remember standing by a round metal table which Helen had dragged to the edge of the canal behind her house. I waited while Helen guided Sally, who was almost blind. They came like two dancers, gliding slowly over the rough lawn. I watched them, barely touching hands, settle on two chairs pulled close to each other. The table was piled with hibiscus and bougainvillea blossoms picked from nearby bushes.

I saw how frail Helen appeared. Her movements reminded me of a stately white heron that sometimes strode up from the canal for handouts. The canal was a green mat of moss-like grass and lilies that was almost an extension of the lawn. Turtles and coots walked and swam on and under the surface.

As I sat down at the table, a mullet shot out of the grassy water into the air. It created a silver arc suspended one, two, three seconds. An anhinga gauged the landing time of the fish and lunged for dinner, but a moment too late. The splash back to safety startled Sally. The fish wriggled out of sight under the mat of grass.

"Ah, everyone is here," Helen said. She looked the length of the canal. It was alive with crawling, swimming, flying, buzzing creatures. The glitter of sunlight dancing on the wet blanket of green made me blink. A cloud of gnats and flies seemed to float motionless in the air before it changed shape. Predatory broad-winged red and blue mosquito hawks patrolled like old World War I fighter planes.

I felt honored that this ceremony had been planned for me. Helen believed in ritual. Great questions, great answers, great resolve had to be celebrated, sung to, spoken to, danced — otherwise, the universe would pay no attention. Mullet and turtles and other creatures would have no faith in our intentions. Helen affirmed that the universe was going somewhere, and to go with it, we had to make our intentions known.

Helen was, above all, practical. She knew that the three of us would never forget that day. I think Helen already understood the personal tragedies that would soon overtake both her and Sally. Helen lit a small container filled with lemon grass. I saw that the container was an old tuna can polished bright with steel wool. She nestled the can among the flowers and a ribbon of pungent smoke drifted out of the bougainvillea blossoms. With a long turkey feather, Helen lifted ribbons of smoke and directed them toward the canal. Sally took a deep breath then began to speak. I was surprised by the integrity of her voice: undramatic, conversational, as though she were addressing me.

"We are two grandmothers," she said. Her gray eyes seemed to drift with the smoke. "We are old. I am almost blind. We were worried about the world that we are leaving to our grandchildren, but something has happened that has given us hope. Something has ended, and a new thing is beginning. That is why we have come here today...."

CELEBRATING A GREAT THING

Sally paused and touched my hand. Helen used the feather to draw a ribbon of smoke toward me. I leaned forward and breathed deeply.

"We have brought a friend," Sally said. "He is a grandfather who shares our concerns. We have brought him with us to celebrate with you a great thing."

Helen spoke a single syllable, "Ho." She moved the feather in a circle above the smoldering lemon grass. Then, slowly, she rose like a heron stretching from its sleep, one muscle at a time. She stood in the stiff stance of a long-legged bird getting ready to strike, or to dance. Carefully, she slid the feather beneath a silver wave in her hair which had been prepared at the beauty parlor for that moment. The feather was like an arrow moving through a cloud, resting in a grandmother's hair.

I felt myself becoming lighter. I extended a cupped hand, drew the smoke toward me and repeated, "Ho!" Helen and Sally giggled. I saw Helen's bird-like posture go limp. She laughed. Sally touched my hand again, pressing it gently against the cold metal table top. I understood, without embarrassment. The women were walking a fine line. Helen did not want me to be light-headed, spaced out. She wanted me here, present to pay attention to every detail.

"We Grandmothers were so organized," Helen said, speaking in the same conversational tone Sally had used. She was speaking to the inhabitants of the canal. "We were old enough to let go. Let go of our attachments. Let go of wanting success. I was hopeful because such women could actually untangle themselves from the false stories that society must tell in order to exist."

MOST MEN PRETEND UNTIL THEY DIE

Helen looked down at me. Her transparent blue eyes, which could be icy, seemed melted with compassion. "The false stories trap men longer than they trap women. I think almost all men go on pretending until they die."

The silver mullet risked flight again. This time the Anhinga was ready — its snake neck struck true. The bird impaled the fish on its beak in midair, a thing I had never seen before. Helen saw it and flinched. We watched, respectfully, as the bird maneuvered up the canal bank to the lawn. Eyeing us, it flipped the wriggling fish into the air and snatched it on its way down, swallowing it whole. With wet black wings outstretched for balance, it waddled back onto the green canopy of the canal, a wet cigar shape still wriggling in its neck.

"So be it. Ho," Helen said and patted Sally's shoulder. "That was not planned. When a teacher is needed, the teacher will appear. That is the way nature works. That is why we are here. A teacher appeared to us. He was a young boy. We are now in a new place because he taught us what we had sought to learn. Even this grandfather has awakened with us."

Helen reached up and drew the feather through her hair as though it were an arrow. She touched me with it and said, "this ceremony is to help the grandfather remember who he is. It is also to remind us that a young grandson taught us who we are. We are no longer in the old story. We no longer think in the old manner."

Helen walked along the edge of the canal. Coots expecting to be fed splashed from all directions toward her. She held the feather behind her like a pitcher ready to throw a ball. She snapped it forward and it caught the breeze. It glided effortlessly past mosquito hawks. Coots paddled wildly in pursuit.

Helen didn't wait to see the feather land or the coots' disappointment. She returned quickly to the table and sat down. She and Sally let their hands touch, barely visible in the flowers.

CHIEFS WHO WILL LISTEN

"Knowing one's story is what matters most," Sally said. "The boy understood that — not the details, but the essentials — at a glance. He understood that the old story was concentrated in him. Billions of years were telescoped into one or two generations. Because he understood we can now understand. All of the past and all of the future is in us, too."

The last of the lemon grass crumpled into ashes. Helen lifted the tin and poured the last smoke into the wind. She watched it disappear molecule after molecule. She began a prayer. "Creator of us all, let our smoke join in the endless stream of smoke of all generations. Let the grandfather and the grandson resolve to raise up a new generation of chiefs who will listen."

Helen and Sally arose like two silver-crested herons rising from sleep, one muscle at a time. I joined them stiffly, and we three embraced. In a shuffling circle, feeling ageless in our old age, we danced our resolve. We sang it. "Ho!"

MEDITATION ON THE OCCASION OF A GRADUATION

Our dance ended and Helen left us. I held Sally's hand to steady her. We waited.

"Welcome, little sister." Helen addressed a moss-back turtle the size of a round green watermelon cut in half. She had just climbed out of the canal. She dug with hind flippers into a bare spot in Helen's lawn. Beads of water dripped from her mossy back like perspiration. As she laid eggs into Earth, the turtle returned Helen's gaze.

Helen began to recite the meditation that we had written together for the occasion of my graduation.

A VIEW OF A SNAIL'S WAY

The day I was born, the day my eyes first blinked light, the day my lungs emerged from the sea of my mother's womb to gulp their first breath of air, on that day, a countdown began.

I, and you, and every living thing are united by a countdown of diminishing numbers. Butterflies count days. Two. One. None. We count years. Diminishing heartbeats. A million million? Boom. Less one. Boom. Less two. How many heartbeats measure my unbelievable gift? With what breath will I learn to believe? What image will awaken me?

A river flows a fixed number of miles to the sea. But the river knows only its flow. We humans, you and I, measure rivers and lives into finite beginnings and endings. Only by measuring, and by listening to our diminishing heartbeats, can we know to ask the questions that make us human.

The butterfly's purpose is to become a caterpillar, not to count. The river's purpose is to flow, not to measure. My purpose, yours and mine, is to count and to measure and to ask: What is my purpose? How did it begin? Where will it end? Why am I here?

In Earth's story, I am here because I am needed. I am needed in this place, in this time. You are needed, too. We are the eyes and the ears of eons of time, of a river of butterflies and of all life. Whatever questions Earth would ask while its heart yet beats, it must ask through us. Earth's questions are our questions, too.

Why Are We Here? Ask R. Buckminster Fuller:

We, you and I, are on the last lap of a long relay race. The race will be touch and go to the very end. If we make it across that ending, we will qualify for the next beginning. "Qualifying" is what we are doing now. We, Earth's brains encased in human skulls, are standing for our final exam. The exam will determine whether we humans, our children, qualify to go on.

What Is Our Purpose? Ask Allen Wheelis:

We are the carriers of Earth's spirit. We did not create spirit, nor can we possess or define it. But we are its bearers. Spirit rises, matter falls. Spirit reaches like a flame, a leap of a dancer. Spirit is a traveller, passing now through the human realm. We inch it forward with each beat of the heart. We falter, pass it on to our children. Spirit passes on, enlarged, enriched, stranger, more complex.

Spirit leaps aside from matter which tugs forever to pull it down, to make it still. Minute creatures writhe in warm oceans. They come together, touch, something passes. Viruses become bacteria, become algae, become ferns. Thrust of Spirit cracks stone, drives up Douglas fir. Amoebas reach out soft blunt arms in ceaseless motion to find the world, to know it better, questing further.

Viewed closely, the path of Spirit is seen to meander, is a glisten of a snail's way in the night forest. But from a height, minor turnings merge into a steadfastness of course. Humans have reached a ledge from which to look back. For thousands of years the view is clear. The horizon is millions of years behind us. Beyond the vagrant turnings of our last march stretches a shining path.

Where Will the Path End? Ask Nikos Kasantzakis:

How shall we confront life and death, virtue and fear? All our race takes refuge in us, asks questions and lies waiting in agony. In this lightning moment when we walk the Earth, our first duty is to live through the endless march, both visible and invisible, of our beings. Our dead do not lie in the ground. They have become birds, trees, air. We sit under their shade. We are nourished by their flesh. We inhale their breathing. They have become our ideas and passions. Myriad hands hold our hands and direct them. When we sleep, tombs open in the memory till our skulls brim with ghosts. We must gather our strength and listen: the whole heart of humanity is a single outcry.

This is the moment of greatest crisis. As soon as we were born, you and I, a new possibility was born with us. We have a great responsibility. We do not govern our own small, insignificant existence. We are the throw of the dice on which, for the moment, the entire fate of our race is gambled.

NOTES

1. Pierre Teilhard de Chardin, "The Spirit of the Earth," in *Human Energy* 39.

2. R. Buckminster Fuller, *Critical Path* (New York: St. Martin's Press, 1981).

3. Allen Wheelis, *On Not Knowing How to Live* (New York: Harper & Row, 1975).

4. Nikos Kasantzakis, *The Saviors of God: Spiritual Exercises* (New York: Simon & Schuster, 1969).

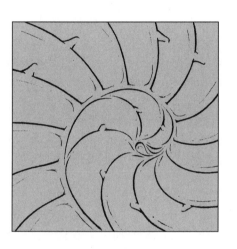

My heart leaps up when I behold
A rainbow in the sky:
So was it when my life began;
So is it now I am a man;
So be it when I shall grow old.
The Child is the father of the Man;
And I could wish my days to be
Bound each to each by natural piety.

William Wordsworth
My Heart Leaps Up When I Behold[1]

EPILOGUE

MY MOST IMPORTANT LESSON

Ben, you taught me my most important lesson. As long as I keep asking myself your question, I keep learning. Now that you know, what are you going to do about it?

The Grandmothers took me to a ledge where I could see millions of years into the past. I could think my way along the glisten of a snail's trail through forests and through galaxies, all the way back to my own beginning. But I still had trouble thinking my way Seven Generations into the future. Because you asked your question, I have stayed awake to the world the Grandmothers helped me to see. The reality is that my species has achieved the power to consume faster than Earth can produce.

You showed us, Ben, that our received version of the way things are is really only a blip on a larger cosmic screen. The day you walked up to the blackboard, you were a carrier of Earth's spirit. We all saw it — Spirit reaching like a flame, the leap of a dancer, Spirit passing through the human realm.

In the larger picture you showed us, we appeared merely to be ancient amoebas reaching out with blunt arms, seeking a world. The reason humankind is consuming Earth is because we are amoebas, but amoebas with intelligence, amoebas with science and technology whose reach exceeds the grasp of our short, soft arms.

You were right: the human species could never have made the transition from primitive amoebas to fully conscious humans unless we discovered the world with our senses, wrestled with it, consumed it. Our greatest asset has become our greatest liability. We have not learned when and where to stop. However, if we are transformed into the beings that we can and should be, we will embrace the world, we will love Earth as an extension of ourselves, and ourselves as an extension of Earth.

Ben, I still catch glimpses of the larger reality you demonstrated for us, but I have to work at remembering what is really going on in the world around us. In the larger reality, what is going on is not the bankruptcy of Earth's economy. It isn't the amoeba-like consumption of Earth's resources by the human species. What is going on is the passing of Spirit through the human realm. Spirit is being enlarged and enriched, it is becoming stranger and more complex.

My glimpses of this larger reality help me to focus on what I must do in response to your question. One thing I must do is to try to curb my participation in the over-consumption of my species, by building a sustainable dwelling made out of bales of straw, for example, or helping to create an Earth Literacy curriculum. By trying to use my own blunt amoeba arms in ways that will destroy less and embrace more.

But the world of my doing is small. When I live only in this world, alone and isolated, I suffer burnout and depression, I lose heart and hope.

Ben, during the few minutes you stood at the blackboard, you gave the Grandmothers and me a gift: the hope that we could do what we saw you doing. If we could follow your lead we would not have to worry about burnout, we would not

be consumed with depression or loss of heart, for you demonstrated the wisdom of all spiritual traditions. You taught us
the art of "being in the world but not of it."

I remember a time when your example made all the
difference to me. I was enrolled in a week-long study on the
practice of prayer. The sponsor was the Academy for Spiritual
Formation[2] at the United Methodist "Upper Room," just a
few blocks from Vanderbilt University in Nashville. Every
four months I would go there for a retreat. The two years I
participated in the Academy were like a postgraduate continuation of the teachings the Grandmothers gave me. Each
session was a lesson in trying to live in the world without
being of it.

In the session I am recalling, we studied Paul's instructions to "pray without ceasing" (I Thes. 5:17). Our
assignment was to create for ourselves a "breath prayer," a
word or phrase that we could tuck into our subconscious to
whisper us back into reality when the distractions of our
small-world living began to overwhelm us. Our goal was to
transform our unconscious breathing process into a conscious
process of meditation. I made lists. I tried short phrases that
would fit into my breathing, words that would remind me to
stay awake. Nothing seemed to work. Frustrated, I decided to
visit the Vanderbilt Divinity School library, hoping that
perhaps a theologian's commentary on incessant prayer could
offer some direction.

On the short drive to the library, the roads were
jammed. I had to wait two cycles at a traffic signal before I
could reach my destination. Staring impatiently at the metal
signal box on the corner, I remained engrossed in the small
world of schedules, goals, and my pressing need to hurry. I
mechanically rehearsed a few candidates from my "breath
prayer" list. Then, I noticed something moving inside the
metal box at which I had been staring. A tuft of straw was

being pulled into the casing, and as it disappeared, the head of a House Sparrow peered out. As the bird's mate arrived with more straw, the sparrow flew out over the crowded line of cars.

In the small world of traffic jams, a flame leaped. The same Spirit that cracks rocks and drives up Douglas firs in the forests was building a nest inside an urban traffic light. When the signal turned green, I pulled onto a side street, parked, and went back to watch. I no longer needed the commentaries of theologians. While I watched from the shade of a brick wall, sucking in fumes of exhaust from idling cars, a pair of small birds offered me my "breath prayer." The binding spell of the small game that I had been playing (a game that had nothing to do with where the universe is going) was broken. The sparrows, unperturbed by the sound and the fury of internal combustion engines and frustrated humans, lifted me to the same ledge where the Grandmothers had once taken me. I could see the horizon millions of years into the past, and for the first time I could see the horizon seven generations into the future.

I noticed my breathing, and I realized that these birds, too, were breathing, as were the frustrated humans rushing by in their cars or hurrying along on the sidewalk. Each of us depended on this action of our lungs, of air flowing in and out. This was indeed a "breath prayer." I felt again the leap of a dancer, a flame rising. Not one of us was telling our lungs to breathe in and breathe out. Without thinking, we were taking into our bodies molecules of life, molecules of matter. We were inhaling and exhaling the universe.

While I matched my breathing with my new prayer, I missed the Academy's next lecture. I was more concerned with a profound truth: I breathe the universe, in and out.

One bird dropped a beak full of straw. It dived to retrieve it just as a car moved forward. At the last minute, the bird changed course, dodged the car, and flew off toward the campus. I held my breath until she was safe. When I began to breathe again, my prayer had changed: The universe breathes me, in and out.

Ben, just as amoebas reach out to know the world, the universe reaches out to know us. It breathes us. When I inhale, the cosmos exhales, filling my lungs. When I exhale, the universe inhales. As I tried to match my breathing to this thought, I became disoriented. The "breath prayer" worked. While physically breathing in, it was difficult to think, "the universe breathes out." The disorientation was just what was needed to shatter my small-world game.

In the larger reality you showed me, I now see that the universe does breathe me. To breathe consciously is to pray. All amoebas, all living beings, "pray without ceasing." The universe breathes us as we breathe the universe. That is what we all do. That is what the universe does.

Thank you, Ben, for being my teacher. I hope that some day you will come stay in my straw-bale house at Narrow Ridge.

Notes

1. William Wordsworth, "My Heart Leaps Up When I Behold," *The Norton Anthology of Poetry*, ed. Arthur M. Eastman, et al (New York: W.W. Norton & Co., 1970) 579.

2. For information about programs offered by the Academy for Spiritual Formation write: P.O. Box 189, Nashville, TN 37202.

APPENDIX

The following is a partial list of Earth Literacy Centers in the eastern United States and South America. Each offers a variety of adult education programs encouraging the exploration of earth literacy concepts.

Crystal Springs
76 Everett Skinner Road
Plainville, MA 02762

Genesis Farm*
41A Silver Lake Road
Blairstown, NJ 07825

Grailville
932 O'Bannonville Rd
Loveland, OH 45140

Homecomings
St. Gabriel's Monastery
631 Griffin Pond Rd.
Clark's Summit, PA 18411

Narrow Ridge Earth Literacy Center
RR#2, Box 125
Washburn, TN 37888

Saint Mary-of-the-Woods College**
Saint Mary-of-the-Woods, IN 47876

Spiritearth
43 Spaulding Lane
Saugertus, NY 12477-2399

Vida Verde Earth Literacy Center***
c/o Sister Patricia Leon
Colegio de San Francisco
Aereo, Apartado 131210
Bogota, Colombia 10121

Western Pennsylvania and Eastern Ohio
Earth Literacy Network
c/o Dr. Gene Wilhelm
513 Kelly Blvd.,
Slippery Rock, PA 16057-1145

* Genesis Farm publishes a quarterly newsletter which features the writings of Sister Miriam Therese MacGillis. A one-year subscription is $10 and may be obtained from the address above.

** St. Mary-of-the Woods has just recently implemented an accredited Master's degree program in Earth Literacy. Students have the opportunity to pursue their study on the college campus, and/or at participating Earth Literacy Centers around the country. For more information, please write to the above address.

*** This Genesis Farm sister community features the Aluna Project, a campaign for preserving portions of Colombia's Darien Rainforest. Earth Literacy students live in native villages and study with indigenous teachers. For information on how you may purchase and preserve one or more acres of the rainforest (starting with a $32 contribution) contact Ana Maria Vasquez at the address above, or send your inquiry via Genesis Farm.

SELECTED BIBLIOGRAPHY FOR FURTHER STUDY

Barnes, Michael, ed. *An Ecology of the Spirit.* Lanham, MD: University Press of America, 1990.

Berry, Thomas. *The Dream of the Earth.* San Francisco: Sierra Club Books, 1988.

Berry, Thomas and Clark, Thomas. *Befriending the Earth.* Mystic, CT: XXIII Publications, 1993.

Berry, Thomas and Swimme, Brian. *The Universe Story.* San Francisco: HarperSanFrancisco, 1992).

Berry, Wendell. *The Gift of Good Land.* San Francisco: North Point Press, 1981.

_____. *The Unsettling of America.* San Francisco: Sierra Club Books, 1977.

_____. *What Are People For?* San Francisco: North Point Press, 1990.

Daly, Hermann and Cobb, John. *For the Common Good.* Boston: Beacon Press, 1989.

Dominquez, Joe and Robin, Vicki. *Your Money or Your Life.* New York: Viking Press, 1988.

Dowd, Michael. *Earthspirit.* Mystic, CT: XXIII Publications, 1991.

Fox, Matthew. *Original Blessing.* Santa Fe, NM: Bear & Company, 1984.

_____. *The Re-Invention of Work.* San Francisco: HarperSanFranciso, 1988.

Hawken, Paul. *The Ecology of Commerce.* New York: Harper Collins, 1994).

Jackson, Wes. *Becoming Native to This Place.* Lexington: University of Kentucky Press, 1995.

Jackson, Wes, et.al. *Meeting the Expectations of the Land.* San Francisco: North Point Press, 1984.

Johnson, Elizabeth. *Women, Earth and Creator Spirit.* Mahwah, NJ: Paulist Press, 1993.

Korten, Robert. *When Corporations Rule the World.* West Hartford, CT: Kumarian Press, 1995).

MacGillis, Miriam Therese. *Our Origin Story: Foundations for Ecological Responsibility.* Kansas City, MO: Sheed and Ward, 64141.

___. "Spirituality and Ecology." *Pax Christi, USA* (Summer, 1994).

Meeker-Lowry, Susan. *Invested in the Common Good.* Philadelphia: New Society Publishers, 1995.

Raymo, Chet. *Honey From Stone.* New York: Penguin Books, 1989.

Robbins, John. *Reclaiming Our Health.* Tiburn, CA: H.J. Dramer, 1996.

Swimme, Brian. *The Universe is a Green Dragon.* Santa Fe, NM: Bear & Company, 1994.

Theobald, Robert. *Reworking Success: New Communities at the Millennium.* Stoney Creek, CT: New Society Publishers, 1997.